UNDERSTANDING ECONOMICS

A CASE STUDY APPROACH

GLOBE FEARON EDUCATIONAL PUBLISHER
A Division of Simon & Schuster
Upper Saddle River, New Jersey

Director of Editorial and Marketing, Secondary Supplementary:
   Nancy Surridge

Project Editors: Carol Schneider, Bernice Golden, and Kirsten Richert

Economics Content Reviewer: Jane S. Lopus, Ph.D., Associate Professor
   of Economics and Director, Center for Economics Education,
   California State University, Hayward

Editorial Developer: Curriculum Concepts, Inc.

Production Director: Kurt Scherwatzky

Production Editor: Rosann Bar

Electronic Page Production: Elaine Kilcullen and José A. López

Photo Research: Jenifer Hixson

Art Direction: Joan Jacobus

Cover Design: Paradigm Design

Interior Design: Kay Wanous

Maps and Technical Illustrations: Siren Design

Photo Credits:
p. 3: Food From the 'Hood; **p. 4:** Food From the 'Hood; **p. 5:** Food From the
'Hood; **p. 6:** Food From the 'Hood; **p. 20:** UPI/Bettman; **p. 22:** Doug Armand, Tony
Stone Images; **p. 23:** W. Niedner; **p. 38:** Courtesy of Domino's; **p. 39:** Bettman;
p. 40: Courtesy of Domino's; **p. 56 :** Lewis Hine, Library of Congress; **p. 58:** Mary
Kate Denny, Photo Edit; **p. 74:** Courtesy of Schwinn Cycling and Fitness Group;
p. 75: Bettman Archive; **p. 76:** Tim Davis/Photo Researchers; **p. 77:** Courtesy of
Schwinn Cycling and Fitness Group; **p. 93:** Scott and Gillian Aldrich;
p. 94: Courtesy of Ben and Jerry's; **p. 95:** © Roland Freeman; **p. 110:** W. Niedner;
p. 112: Courtesy of Air France; **p. 113:** W. Niedner; **p. 128:** Scott and Gillian
Aldrich; **p. 130:** ©John Coletti, Stock Boston; **p. 146:** Melanie Carr/ Zephyr
Pictures; **p. 147:** W. Niedner; **p. 148:** Andy Levin, Photo Researchers;
p. 164: The Bettman Archive; **p. 166:** Courtesy of Coca-Cola;
p. 167: Owen Franken, Stock Boston

Printed in the United States of America
   4 5 6 7 8 9 10   98 99 00 01

B88
ISBN 0-8359-1810-6

CURR
HB 5
171.5
U52
.1998

GLOBE FEARON EDUCATIONAL PUBLISHER
A Division of Simon & Schuster
Upper Saddle River, New Jersey

CONTENTS

Welcome to *Understanding Economics: A Case Study Approach*. Each of the ten chapters in this book begins with a case study followed by a worktext. The case studies look at real-life situations involving economics. The worktexts discuss the economic concepts in the case studies. Questions and activities throughout the worktexts will help you learn important economic principles.

Why is it important for you to learn about economics? Understanding economics can help you get the best deal on a CD player, a raise from your boss, or a loan for a used car.

Without economic skills, it's difficult to understand our ever-changing world. Life bombards us with information about inflation, unemployment, the stock market, and international trade. If you understand economics, you can analyze what you read and hear. Then you can decide what's best for your economic future—just like the students at Crenshaw High School did.

The Crenshaw High students pictured below are the subjects of the Chapter 1 case study. They are the student owners of Food From the 'Hood, a South Central Los Angeles natural foods company. These students learned basic economic concepts that helped them to become successful business owners.

Remember, a strong foundation in economics is the first step to a successful future.

CASE STUDY: FOOD FROM THE 'HOOD

It's March 1994. The Natural Food Products Show is taking place in Anaheim, California. A 15-year-old high school student is making a sales pitch at her company's booth. An interested group of people gathers. They are clearly impressed by the student and her product. What company does she work for? What product is she selling?

The company is called Food From the 'Hood. Its commercial product is salad dressing. The young woman is not only a great salesperson, but she's also an owner of the company! Food From the 'Hood is the first student-owned and student-run natural foods company in the United States. Its business address is Crenshaw High School, South Central Los Angeles, California.

How can a community recover its hope?

Rebuilding a Community

Food From the 'Hood was started as a result of the May 1992 Los Angeles riots. The riots were devastating to South Central and West Los Angeles. Businesses were burned. Grocery stores were looted. Homes were destroyed. Neighborhood people who worked in local businesses lost their jobs. The community seemed to have lost hope.

How could the community recover its hope? This was a big question in the mind of Tammy Bird. A biology teacher at Crenshaw High School, Bird had an idea involving an empty lot behind the high school. She wanted to turn the lot into a vegetable garden. Students would work in the garden to grow food. The food grown in the garden could be donated to needy people in the neighborhood. Bird shared her idea with several students. They were excited about this chance to help their community.

In addition to helping the community, Bird believed the garden would help the students. Creating a garden would give them valuable hands-on science experience. The students who volunteered to work on the project were offered extra credit in science.

An excited group of students got to work. As they cleared and weeded the lot, they realized that they had several decisions to make. They had to decide which vegetables to grow. They needed to figure out what methods they should use to grow the vegetables. They even needed to decide where to donate the food.

The students discovered that there was much that they needed to learn. They went to the library to do research. They researched how to plant a vegetable garden. They discovered which vegetables would grow best in Los Angeles. They learned about organic gardening. In an organic garden, plants are grown without pesticides or chemical fertilizers.

After a great deal of reading and talking, the students came up with a plan. They would plant lettuce, cabbage, collard greens, squash, tomatoes, and broccoli. They also decided to plant some herbs, including thyme, parsley, and basil. They decided to grow the food organically. Finally, they decided that they would donate the crop to a local food bank, Helpers for the Homeless and the Hungry. Students spent extra hours at the lot making their plan a reality.

Birth of a Business

Crenshaw High School's garden caught the attention of a local newspaper reporter. The reporter wrote an article about it. The article captured the interest of a woman named Melinda McMullen. McMullen worked in public relations for

Students painted their statement of purpose for the garden. A statement of purpose helps a business set its priorities.

STATEMENT OF PURPOSE

1. CREATE JOBS.
2. GIVE BACK TO THE COMMUNITY.
3. PROTECT THE ENVIRONMENT.
4. LEARN FROM OUR EXPERIENCE
5. SHOW WHAT WE CAN ACCOMPLISH.
6. BE PROFITABLE.

businesses in the Los Angeles area. After the riot, she wanted to get involved in a recovery project in South Central Los Angeles. She thought that the garden was a great idea. McMullen volunteered her help immediately.

McMullen met with the students. She asked them, "Why not start a business?" The students could sell the vegetables they grew. They could use the profits to start a college scholarship fund. McMullen said that one way to give power to the students was to give them a stake in the business. All students who worked in the garden would become student owners of the business.

The students were excited by McMullen's suggestion. The idea of starting a business called for more decisions. The students wondered where they would sell their food. They had to decide what prices to charge. To help make these decisions, the students first described their company:

- We are a student-owned business.

- We are in the food business.

- We are headquartered in the inner city.

- We are a multicultural company.

They also developed a statement of purpose.

Now the business needed a name. The students brainstormed a list of 72 names. They narrowed the list to five "finalist" names. Then the students talked to various people about the five names. The name that everyone liked the most was Food From the 'Hood. It was catchy. It was fun. The name identified the product. It also told people where the students were from. *'Hood* is slang for "inner-city neighborhood."

Now the business had a name. It was time to create a logo. A logo is a picture or a symbol that makes people think of a certain company. The students created a logo that would make people think of Food From the 'Hood as a student-run, multicultural business from the inner city.

Time to Harvest

On December 18, 1992, when Food From the 'Hood harvested its first crop. The students stuck to their original plan of donating all the garden vegetables to Helpers for the Homeless and the Hungry. The next harvest would be devoted to the scholarship fund.

Straight Out 'the Garden®

During the next school term, students worked very hard. The company got a huge boost from the State of California Riot Recovery Fund. The fund donated $49,000 to help students learn the basic business skills needed to run a successful company. The donation made it possible for Melinda McMullen to quit her public relations job and work full-time with Food From the 'Hood.

The next crop was harvested in July 1993. This time, the students sold their herbs and vegetables at a local farmers' market. Their products were a huge

success. Within 30 minutes, the students sold $150 worth of vegetables! The students continued selling their crops.

By September, they had earned $600 in profits. Profit is the money that a business makes after all costs have been paid. The money was used to give college scholarships to three students. It wasn't a lot of money, but it helped. Food From the 'Hood wanted to give even more scholarships, but they had to find a way to raise more money.

Out 'the Garden Into a Bottle

One of the problems faced by the students of Food From the 'Hood was that they could only grow a limited amount of food on the quarter-acre lot. This limited the amount of money that the company could make. The students needed to think of another way to make money. With help from McMullen, the students decided to create a salad dressing.

The students contacted Rebuild Los Angeles (RLA). RLA was the city's riot recovery agency. RLA suggested that Food From the 'Hood contact Sweet Adelaide Enterprises. Sweet Adelaide is a female-owned business and is a leading salad dressing packer in the Los Angeles area. Sweet Adelaide agreed to manufacture and bottle the dressing.

In December 1993, Food From the 'Hood got a huge surprise. RLA awarded the company a $50,000 grant. The grant helped the company set up offices and begin developing a product. Now it was time to create a recipe for the salad dressing.

Over the next few months, the students experimented with six recipes. They tried to get just the right balance of basil and parsley. Finally, the students created just the right balance of ingredients. Their home-made recipe for creamy Italian dressing was ready for mass production. They named it Straight Out 'the Garden. Now they needed to figure out how and where to sell their new salad dressing.

Word of the new dressing leaked out to the salad dressing industry. Norris Bernstein was one of the first to hear the news. Bernstein's family had run a successful restaurant and salad dressing business for many years. He contacted Food From the 'Hood and volunteered his time. With his help, the students set a financial goal. Their goal was to earn $50,000 after business expenses and taxes. They figured out that they would have to sell 30,000 cases of salad dressing to reach their goal.

Bernstein introduced the students to some of the leaders in the supermarket industry. With his help, the students set out to reach their distribution goal. They showed their product to local grocers, as well as to large supermarket chains. Representatives from the stores were impressed. Within two months, every major grocery chain in the Los Angeles area agreed to carry the dressing. In April 1994, Straight Out 'the Garden hit the shelves. People bought it. People liked it. It

A student plants seedlings in the garden. Food From the 'Hood began as a small volunteer project. Students expected extra credit in science. They got much more! They became student-owners of a successful business.

sold very well, and sales have continued to be very successful.

The success of Straight Out 'the Garden can be partially measured in numbers. By May 1995, Straight Out 'the Garden had greatly expanded its selling territory. The dressing was being sold in over 2,000 grocery and natural food stores in 23 states. The company has sold thousands of cases of dressing. Expected profits in 1995 were estimated to reach the students' goal of $50,000.

Into the Future

The success of Food From the 'Hood can also be measured in other ways. The number of students in Food From the 'Hood who have been accepted at four-year colleges is rising. In 1995, 10 of the 15 seniors were accepted at four-year colleges. All of the 15 seniors were awarded Food From the 'Hood scholarships. To help students prepare for college, Food From the 'Hood set up a program that offers college counseling and after-school tutoring to students at Crenshaw High School. The program also offers a study course for the SATs. The students also remain committed to their community. They continue to give 25 percent of their produce to feed needy people.

In the meantime, students still work in the garden behind the high school. They still sell their produce at farmers' markets. Between sales, they talk about their futures. One of the students wants to be an

Students put in extra hours working in the garden in order to meet their business goals.

art director. Another student wants to go into international business.

Food From the 'Hood was a small project at the beginning. The students started out by clearing an overgrown lot to earn extra credit. They didn't know much about gardening. They knew even less about running a business. All that has changed. They are successful business people and well-respected in their community. Food From the 'Hood makes a profit and has gained a national following. More important than the money is the sense of accomplishment that the students feel. They showed that inner-city kids could and did make a difference.

What Is Economics?

Jaynell Grayson is a senior at Crenshaw High School in South Central Los Angeles. Let's take a look at what Grayson does during a school day and see how economics affects her life. She lives with her grandfather. Every day, she takes three buses to get to school. Once at school, she goes to her classes. She also works a certain number of hours each week at Food From the 'Hood. As one of the student owners, she has a responsibility to take part in running the company. Her tasks might include taking orders, working in the garden, attending sales meetings, or writing letters. After school, Grayson bags groceries to make extra money.

What part does economics play in Grayson's day? To answer this question, we need to define economics. **Economics** is the study of how people choose to use their limited resources to produce goods and services. **Goods** are products that people use. For example, vegetables, herbs, and salad dressing are goods that Grayson helps Food From the 'Hood produce. **Services** are activities that people do for other people. When students take orders for their salad dressing, answer the telephone, or write letters, they are providing a service.

1. What is economics?

_____

_____

2. What are goods?

_____

_____

3. What are services?

_____

_____

At the Food From the 'Hood offices, the students use many services to help them produce their goods. They use the services of the electric company for electricity. They use the phone company and an on-line service provider for their computers. They also use the services of adults and professionals who are experts in various areas of the business world.

4. List three goods that Food From the 'Hood produces.

_____

_____

_____

5. List three services that Food From the 'Hood might use.

_____

_____

_____

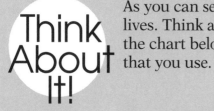

As you can see, economics plays a very important part in people's lives. Think about the various goods and services that you use. In the chart below, list the names of three goods and three services that you use.

Goods	Services
6. _____	_____
7. _____	_____
8. _____	_____

Economics is also about the choices that people make. The basic economic problem facing individuals, as well as entire societies, is the problem of scarcity. **Scarcity** occurs when people want more goods and services than they can have. You will learn more about scarcity later in this chapter. Because of scarcity, people must make choices about how to best use their limited resources. For example, one scarce resource facing Food From the 'Hood was the amount of land available to them. Because the amount of land was limited, students had to make a choice about the best way to use it. They decided to grow vegetables organically. This was an economic decision.

Microeconomics and Macroeconomics

Sometimes the study of economics is divided into two separate subjects: microeconomics and macroeconomics. **Microeconomics** is the study of economic decision-making by individuals and businesses. It focuses on prices and output in individual markets for goods and services. Students from Food From the 'Hood made a microeconomic decision when they decided how much to charge for their salad dressing. **Macroeconomics** is the study of the economy as a whole. When you study about inflation or unemployment in the whole economy, you are studying macroeconomics.

9. What is the difference between microeconomics and macroeconomics?

_____

_____

_____

_____

_____

Wants and Needs

Review your list on page 8 of the goods that you use. Which goods do you think are absolutely necessary? Which goods could you do without? The things that people cannot do without are called **needs**. Air, water, food, shelter, and clothing are basic human needs. The things that people desire, but do not need, are called **wants**. Some wants might be a personal computer or a CD player. The needs of all people are basically the same. Wants can be very different from one person to the next. On the chart below, list at least five wants and five needs that you have.

Needs	**Wants**
10. _____	_____
11. _____	_____
12. _____	_____
13. _____	_____
14. _____	_____

Look at the wants that you listed. Because of the economic problem of scarcity, most people cannot have everything that they want. They have to make choices about which wants they will satisfy and which they can do without.

Sometimes the things that people want are closely tied to their needs. For example, Dennis Fomond, one of the students at Food From the 'Hood, wants to go to college. He plans to own a restaurant some day. Getting an education will help him develop more business skills. Owning a restaurant will provide the income that Fomond must have to meet his needs of food, clothing, and shelter, as well as whatever his wants are.

15. How are needs and wants different?

_____

_____

16. Give an example of something you want that you think is closely tied to your needs.

_____

_____

✔ *Check Your Understanding*

Read this paragraph and answer the questions that follow.

Ben Osborn gets up very early to make sure that he arrives at Crenshaw High School by 7:00. It's a nice Saturday in June, and Osborn is working at Food From the 'Hood. Osborn spends the next several hours picking, bundling, and packing vegetables. Then he works with the other students to load the vegetables and salad dressing into cars. The next stop is the Santa Monica Farmers' Market. After setting up the booth, Osborn starts his pitch to the customers: "Tasty and good, it's Food From the 'Hood."

17. What goods do the students take to the market?

_____

_____

18. What services does Osborn perform to get the vegetables ready?

_____

_____

19. What is one service that the students provide at the farmers' market?

_____

_____

Productive Resources

Productive resources, also called **factors of production**, are the resources that people use to create goods and services. For example, land in the empty lot behind Crenshaw High School is a resource because the soil can be used to grow vegetables and herbs. Some resources are made from other resources. For example, soil is used to grow basil and parsley. Basil and parsley are used to make salad dressing. Salad dressing is a good that people want.

Productive resources fall into three basic categories: natural resources, human resources, and capital resources. **Natural resources** are those that are found in nature. Soil, minerals, water, plants, and animals are all natural resources.

There are two types of natural resources: renewable and nonrenewable. A **renewable resource** is one that can be replaced. Trees, water, and animals are some renewable resources. **Nonrenewable resources** cannot be replaced. Minerals, petroleum, and natural gas are some nonrenewable resources. Once they have been used up, those resources are gone forever.

20. What is a resource?

_____

_____

21. List the two types of natural resources.

_____

_____

Human resources include the physical and mental labor that people use to produce goods and services. Human resources also refers to the skills and ideas that people have. Let's look at the human resources used by Food From the 'Hood to produce its goods. Melinda McMullen's skill as a marketing consultant is a human resource. Tammy Bird's skill as a teacher is a human resource. Food From the 'Hood would not be the success that it is without the skills, ideas, and energy of the students. The students are a very important human resource.

Human resources are sometimes divided into two categories: labor and entrepreneurs. **Labor** refers to the workers who work for a business. **Entrepreneurs** are the people responsible for starting up new businesses and introducing new products. Being an entrepreneur involves more than having an idea for a company. It involves risk. The biggest risk that entrepreneurs take is investing money to start the company. The risk for the entrepreneurs is that their business may not be successful. If the business fails, the entrepreneur will probably lose money.

On the other hand, entrepreneurs may profit from the risks that they take. If entrepreneurs introduce a new product or service and the company is successful, the entrepreneurs will probably earn money.

Capital resources are goods made by people that are used to create other goods and services. Tools, such as the garden tools that the students use, are capital resources. The telephones and computers that the students use are also capital resources. Capital resources made from other resources are sometimes called human-made resources.

Most of the goods and services that people use are a combination of capital, natural, and human resources. For example, a garden tool is made in a factory, and a factory is a capital resource. Part of the tool probably came from a natural resource, such as a tree. The skill and labor it took to make the garden tool is a human resource.

TAKE ANOTHER LOOK

Resources Used by Food From the 'Hood

Natural	Human	Capital
soil	Melinda	hoes
air	Tammy	telephones
water	students	computers

22. What are some natural resources used by Food From the 'Hood?

_____

_____

23. What are some human resources used by Food From the 'Hood?

_____

_____

24. What are some capital resources used by Food From the 'Hood?

_____

_____

25. Pick one of the resources listed above. Could Food From the 'Hood be successful without this resource? Explain.

_____

_____

26. What are productive resources?

_____

_____

_____

27. How can entrepreneurs succeed in a business?

_____

_____

_____

28. Why would the students at Crenshaw High School be considered successful "entrepreneurs"?

_____

_____

_____

Production of a Product

Companies use resources to create or produce certain goods and services. Sometimes a company calls upon the services of another company to help it. For example, the entrepreneurs who started Food From the 'Hood did not know how to bottle salad dressing, but they found a company that knew how. The students found Sweet Adelaide Enterprises. Food From the 'Hood contacted Sweet Adelaide because it was well-known for its production of salad dressing. With Sweet Adelaide's help and expertise, Food From the 'Hood was able to create a new product—a product that many people like and buy. The sum total of all the methods that a company uses to create goods and services is referred to as its **production** of the product.

29. What does the term _production_ describe?

_____

_____

_____

30. How did Sweet Adelaide help in the production of Food From the 'Hood's salad dressing?

_____

_____

_____

31. Why did Food From the 'Hood need Sweet Adelaide?

_____

_____

_____

Decisions About Resources

The owners of Food From the 'Hood constantly have to make choices about how to use their resources because all resources are limited, or scarce. The lot that the students use is a quarter acre. A great deal of thought goes into choosing what to grow. The students also have to decide how much of their produce to sell and how much to give to needy people. The decisions that the students make affect their income. Their income, in turn, affects how many scholarships they are able to give each year.

Limitations on Resources

You read earlier that scarcity occurs when people want more goods and services than they can have. Only so much of any good can be produced. Because needs and wants are greater than the available resources, there is a problem. Scarcity requires people to make choices about how to use goods and services to satisfy their wants and needs.

32. What is scarcity?

_____

_____

_____

The Four Basic Economic Questions

You have learned that resources are limited. Therefore, it is in a society's best interest to make the most of the resources that it has. This is what economics is all about. As a result, every economics system in the world must address four basic questions:

- What goods and services will be produced?
- How will these goods and services be produced?
- How much, or how many, of these goods and services will be produced?
- Who will get the goods and services that are produced?

The ways these four economic questions are answered affects how people in a society live. A goal of the owners of Food From the 'Hood was to provide scholarships. It was necessary for the students to answer the four basic economic questions in order to decide how they would reach this goal.

In answering each question, the students had to consider their resources. They had to address the problem of scarcity because their resources were limited. To be successful, they constantly had to make economic choices.

For every choice the students made, they gave up other options. The students faced trade-offs. A **trade-off** is what happens when one choice is exchanged for another. For instance, the students made the choice to spend a lot of time working in the garden and in the offices of Food From the 'Hood. They could have spent time with friends,

---

✔ Check Your Understanding

Review the four basic economic questions. Then use the production of Food From the 'Hood's salad dressing to answer the questions. Refer to the case study if necessary.

33. What does Food From the 'Hood produce?

_____

_____

_____

34. How does Food From the 'Hood produce the salad dressing?

_____

_____

_____

35. How many cases does Food From the 'Hood want to produce?

_____

_____

_____

36. Who gets the salad dressing that Food From the 'Hood produces?

_____

_____

_____

listening to music, or spent time shopping. The students made a choice between leisure time and their business goals.

37. Give an example of a recent trade-off that you faced.

_____

_____

_____

_____

_____

You can also look at trade-offs in another way. Every choice that you make has a cost. Economists look at **cost** as what you give up, or sacrifice, when you make an economic choice. Called opportunity cost or **alternative cost**, every trade-off has this cost. For example, when the students decided to work in the garden on Saturdays, the students gave up other things that they could have done in that time period. Working would contribute to the success of the company. What was given up is called the opportunity cost or alternative cost. Alternative costs must always be considered when making good economic decisions.

38. How do economist define cost, or alternative cost?

_____

_____

_____

_____

39. Why must people always consider alternative costs?

_____

_____

_____

_____

40. What might some of the alternative costs have been for the students who decided to work in the garden on Saturdays?

_____

_____

_____

_____

Reading a Bar Graph

A bar graph can help you compare pieces of information quickly. The bar graph below shows the monthly sales for Straight Out 'the Garden salad dressing. By using the graph, you can quickly compare how many cases were sold from January 1995 to June 1995.

Monthly Sales for Straight Out 'the Garden, 1995

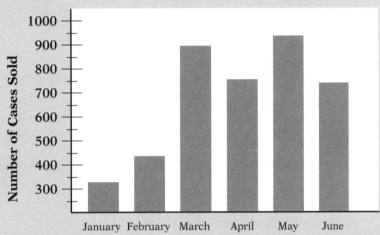

Read the title and the labels to see what information the graph shows. To find out how many cases of salad dressing were sold in January, find January along the bottom of the bar graph. Now look at the top of the bar for that month. Match the top of the bar with the number of cases sold along the left side of the graph. You can see that more than 300 cases of salad dressing were sold in January.

Use the graph to answer the following questions.

1. About how many cases of salad dressing were sold in February?

_____

2. In which month was the most salad dressing sold?

_____

3. About how many more cases were sold in May than in April?

_____

4. About how many cases of salad dressing were sold during the first six months of 1995?

_____

Vocabulary

Complete each sentence with a term from the list below.

factors of production	trade-off	wants	services
natural resources	needs	goods	entrepreneurs

1. Products that people use are called _____.

2. Activities that people do for others are called _____.

3. Things that people desire are _____.

4. Air, water, shelter, and food are basic human _____.

5. The three types of resources are called productive resources,

   or _____.

6. People who start companies are _____.

7. Two types of _____ are renewable
   and nonrenewable resources.

8. When people exchange one choice for another, they face

   a _____.

Main Idea

Complete the following items.

9. What is economics?

   _____

   _____

10. Define scarcity.

    _____

    _____

11. What are the four basic economic questions?

    _____

    _____

    _____

    _____

Understanding Economics

12. Suppose you and a friend decided to make and sell T-shirts with a slogan on them. Explain how each of the four factors of production would be used to make the T-shirts.

13. Suppose you have $20 to spend. List several items that you might want to buy. Decide which item you would purchase. Then explain the trade-off that you faced.

Project

With a group of classmates, discuss a business that you would like to start. Think about what goods or services you would like to provide. What qualities do you want people to associate with your company? Then work together to develop and write a statement of purpose. In the photograph on page 3, look at the statement of purpose that the students of Food From the 'Hood wrote. Use a separate sheet of paper to write your statement of purpose.

It's a sunny afternoon in New York City. The Greenwich Village street is crowded and noisy. That pleases Geng Wong. People walk into the Jang Lok News Store and walk out with purchases. That pleases Geng Wong, too. Business is good. If you were to ask Geng about the store's name, Jang Lok News, you would find out that it is named after a small town in the Fujian province in southern China. Jang Lok is where the Wong family lived in China. The name is a reminder of their faraway first home and the long journey that the family has made, not only in miles but in lifestyle changes.

Geng is the oldest of the three Wong brothers who run the four Jang Lok News stores. Geng and his brothers work from 5 A.M. to 8 P.M., six days a week. The brothers work hard so that they can open more stores and make life more comfortable for their big family. Geng believes that "If you work hard enough and find the right direction in America, you can succeed and make enough money to start even more businesses."

In Geng's hometown of Jang Lok, there was no opportunity

How does economic freedom help small businesses?

to start a business. According to Geng, the Wong family was one of the poorest families in Jang Lok. Though everyone in the family worked very hard, they barely made enough to survive. When Geng was just a child, the Chinese government told people where they would work and what their salaries would be. If the Wong family had tried to start a small business in their town, they would have been accused of "going against the government," Geng said. The penalty would have been a fine or, more likely, jail.

In his U.S. store, Geng makes all of the decisions: what he will sell, how much of each item he will buy, how much he will

Growing up in China during the 1960s was especially difficult for the Wong family. At that time, the Chinese government made all the economic decisions.

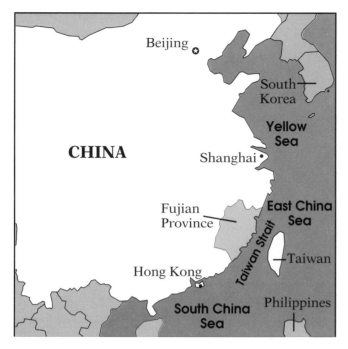

Map showing CHINA with labels: Beijing, South Korea, Yellow Sea, Shanghai, Fujian Province, East China Sea, Taiwan Strait, Taiwan, Hong Kong, South China Sea, Philippines

charge, and what hours he will stay open. "In China," he said, "we couldn't do anything on our own."

A Difficult Life

Geng Wong's parents met and married in Jang Lok in the 1950s. They raised seven children under difficult conditions. Mrs. Wong worked for a construction company. Her job was to move cement, sand, and rocks in a one-wheel wagon. When her five boys grew old enough, they helped her push the heavy wagon. Mr. Wong worked for a local factory as a chef. He cooked lunch for the factory workers.

The Wong children, in addition to helping their mother at her job, would often go into the nearby mountains to cut and collect firewood. They carried the firewood back to town to sell to neighbors. The children also collected bottles and cans to sell. Despite all of the family's hard work, the Wongs remained very poor.

Growing up during the 1960s was especially hard on the Wong family. Economic times were difficult in China. Often, the family didn't have enough to eat. To ease their hunger, they would sometimes eat the husks from rice grains. The Wongs would make these husks more appetizing by mixing them with a little flour and a few vegetables. Eggs, meat, and cooking oil were in short supply. The Chinese government handed out ration coupons for these foods. People could only buy these items when they had coupons for them. Coupons were very difficult to get.

A Closely Controlled Economy

China's economy was strictly controlled by its government when the Wong family lived there. The leaders in the capital city of Beijing made all the economic rules. They decided where factories would be built and what those factories would produce. The leaders also decided to whom those factories would sell their products and how much could be charged for them. The government decided where people would work and how much people would get paid. It also rationed what products people could buy.

The government leaders controlled farming throughout China. The Chinese government owned all of the land and decided which crops would be grown. It assigned groups of families to work an area of farm land together. It then took most of what these collective farms produced and distributed it to the Chinese people.

Economic Migrants

The entire Wong family—especially Mrs. Wong—dreamed of leaving China because of all these government controls. Mrs. Wong had a sister who had moved, or immigrated, to Hong Kong. With her sister's help, Mrs. Wong also moved to Hong Kong. She took along four of her children. The other children stayed behind in Jang Lok with their father.

Hong Kong, though part of Chinese territory, has been under British rule since 1842. The British signed a treaty to return Hong Kong to Chinese rule in 1997. The British did not control Hong Kong's economy with a "tight hand" like the Chinese control their economy. In Hong Kong, Mrs. Wong could work at any job that she was offered. First, she worked as a seamstress. Then she worked in a watch factory. Mrs. Wong was very happy in Hong Kong. She was finally making enough money to take care of her family. More importantly, Mrs. Wong believed that her children now had a future.

After four years apart, the family was finally reunited when Mr. Wong and the three children immigrated to Hong Kong. But their time in Hong Kong would be short. Mei, the eldest daughter, and her husband Henry had immigrated to the United States several years earlier. Mei and Henry had worked hard and saved their money. Finally, they were able to open a newspaper store in downtown New York City.

Coming to America

In 1987, Geng followed his sister to New York. His two younger brothers, Lok and Kang, stayed in Hong Kong to finish high school. When Geng arrived, Mei put him right to work. He had to learn a new language. He had to learn how to do business in the United States. This was new to him because in China the government owned all the businesses and told people how to run them. Geng worked hard to learn the business that Mei and Henry had established.

The following year, 1988, Lok and Kang came to the United States to go to college. Soon, all three brothers had joined Mei

The busy streets of British-ruled Hong Kong offer freedom and opportunity to Chinese immigrants.

and Henry to work in the newspaper store. Their hard work brought them success. After a few years, Mei and Henry moved the business to a bigger store a block away. Now they could sell not only newspapers, but also stationery supplies and other items.

Working in the new store allowed each of the Wong brothers to build up his savings. When each brother saved enough money, he then opened his own store. The Wong brothers now have four stores in lower Manhattan. Mei and Henry have moved into the importing business. They now import products from Beijing.

Mei, Henry, Geng, Lok, and Kang are now citizens of the United States. Their parents have also come to America. Whenever possible, they help out at the stores. Mrs. Wong often gets up at 4:30 A.M. to meet the newspaper delivery person at Lok's store. Then she keeps an eye on the papers until Lok arrives to open the store. Mr. Wong still likes to cook and often brings lunch and dinner to his sons.

The Wongs hope to open more stores. Eventually, they'd like to open larger stores and to hire people from various cultures. Geng says that he would like to give other people the opportunity that he was given when he arrived in the United States—to be able to work hard, save some money, and then start a business.

Economic freedom helps entrepreneurs like the Wongs start businesses in the United States.

What Is An Economic System?

When the Wong family moved from China to the United States, they were amazed by the differences between the economies of the two countries. As you read in this case study, the government in China used to own all the businesses. It also told people where to work. In the United States, people own their own businesses and decide where they want to work. China and the United States have very different economic systems. An **economic system** is the way in which a society decides how to use its resources to produce and distribute goods and services.

Types of Economic Systems

Throughout the world, there are various kinds of economic systems. Each system has advantages and disadvantages. All countries have limited resources. These limitations force them to make economic decisions. The decisions are based on the four basic economic questions that you read about in Chapter 1. They are:

- What goods and services will be produced?
- How will they be produced?
- How much will be produced?
- Who will use the goods and services?

1. What is an economic system?

_____

_____

2. Write one way that the economic system in China is different from that in the United States.

_____

_____

There are three basic economic systems in the world. They are:

- tradition-based economic system
- command economic system
- market economic system

Tradition-based Economy Economic decisions are based largely on custom in a **tradition-based economic system**. The four basic economic questions are answered according to the traditions of that country. People produce and distribute goods in the ways that have been followed for hundreds of years. One advantage of a tradition-based economic system is that it is stable. People simply continue to do what they have done in the past. But there is a big disadvantage to a tradition-based economic system. This kind of economic system does not adapt quickly to change. As a result, it does not usually create rapid economic growth.

3. What is a tradition-based economic system?

_____

_____

4. What is an advantage of a tradition-based economic system?

_____

_____

5. What is a disadvantage of a tradition-based economic system?

_____

_____

There are no countries today that have entirely tradition-based economic systems, but there are communities within countries that have tradition-based economic systems. For example, there is a group of Christians called the Amish that live in farm communities in the United States. Some of their largest communities are in Pennsylvania and Ohio. The Amish have a tradition-based economic system. They grow crops and often sell their goods at farmers' markets in nearby cities. They continue to till the soil with horse-drawn plows. This is the same manner in which they have farmed for hundreds of years.

6. What evidence indicates that the Amish economic system is a tradition-based system?

_____

_____

7. Can you name a community, other than the Amish, that has a tradition-based economic system? Explain why you think that the economic system of this group is tradition-based?

_____

_____

Command Economic System In a pure **command economic system**, a central agency—usually the government—owns and controls the factors of production and decides which goods the country will produce and how the products will be distributed. For example, when the Wong family lived in China, the central government in Beijing decided what the factory where Mr. Wong worked would produce. It also decided where the products would be distributed. Mr. Wong and the other workers did not have any say in these decisions. The Chinese government made all of the country's economic decisions.

A command economic system has its advantages. Citizens are supposed to be taken care of by the government. This may give people an increased sense of security. It also has disadvantages. One disadvantage is that people have little chance to make economic decisions for themselves. As Geng points out, the Wong family could not have opened its own newspaper store in China unless the government decided that it could. Another disadvantage is that people's needs are not always met. As Geng also points out, the Wong family often didn't have enough to eat.

Command economic systems usually occur in dictatorships—communist, facist, or military.

8. What is a command economic system?

_____

9. What is an advantage of a command economic system?

_____

_____

10. What is a disadvantage of a command economic system?

_____

_____

Market Economic System In a **market economic system**, individual people and businesses decide what, how, and how much they will produce and how the products will be distributed. A market economic system is also called free enterprise or capitalism. **Capitalism** is an economic system in which individuals, or capitalists, own and control the factors of production. Remember, you learned in Chapter 1 that the factors of production are natural resources, human resources, and capital resources.

There are a number of advantages and disadvantages to a market economic system. One big advantage is that people are free to make personal economic decisions for themselves. They can act in their own interest. This kind of system encourages people to create a wide variety of goods and services. People can also decide what kind of work they want to do or if they want to be entrepreneurs. For example, Geng and his brothers were free to look for jobs or start any kind of business that they wanted when they came to the United States.

One disadvantage of the market economic system is that some people may not feel as secure as in the other two systems because the government is not always there to help if their business fails or if they lose their job. A pure market economic system is the opposite of a pure command system. The government does not interfere in a pure market system. For example, after filling out the necessary forms and getting approval, Mei and Henry were free to start a business in the United States. However, if their business fails, they will lose the money, time, and work that they put into their business—and the government will not give them new jobs.

11. What is a market economic system?

_____

_____

12. What is an advantage of a market economic system?

_____

_____

_____

13. What is a disadvantage of a market economic system?

_____

_____

14. How does a command economic system differ from a market economic system?

_____

_____

15. In which types of governments do command economic systems usually occur?

_____

_____

_____

✔ Check Your Understanding

Read this paragraph and answer the questions that follow.

Marianna wants to open a cake shop. Everyone in her small town really likes Marianna's cakes. But the government won't let her open a shop. It has found Marianna a job working in a factory that makes sweaters. Marianna wants to make her own economic decisions. She doesn't want the government making them for her.

16. What kind of economic system does the above paragraph describe?

_____

_____

17. What helped you to know what kind of economic system is being described above? Explain.

_____

_____

18. Which economic system do you think Marianna would prefer? Explain why.

_____

_____

Mixed Economic System While the economic systems discussed above are useful models, it is important to realize that no economy is entirely a tradition, command, or market system. Instead, economists agree that today all economic systems are mixed. A **mixed economic system** is one that has some features from tradition, command, and market economic systems. The balance of this mix varies from one country to another.

For example, China's economy is still primarily a command economy. But, in recent years, the government has given citizens a few market-economy freedoms. Chinese farmers may now sell some of their surplus crops to anyone that they want to. China's economic system may be becoming mixed.

19. What is a mixed economic system?

_____

_____

Think About It!

Think about the various economic systems that exist in the world. Then, in the chart below, write how economic decisions are made in each system.

ECONOMIC SYSTEMS	
TRADITION-BASED	**COMMAND**
_____ _____	_____ _____
MARKET	**MIXED**
_____ _____	_____ _____

The word *market* usually refers to a place where people buy and sell products. Economists use this word a bit differently. When economists say **market**, they are referring to the actions of buying and selling. People who buy products are called consumers, or **buyers.** People who sell products are called producers, or **sellers**. Buyers and sellers do business with each other, based on who best satisfies their wants and needs. Today buyers and sellers do business all over the world.

For example, Mei and Henry decided to buy products from sellers in Beijing, China. Mei and Henry have never met the people in Beijing with whom they do business. They conduct their business in a global, or world, market by using telephones, fax machines, and computers. On the other hand, Geng, Lok, and Jang conduct their business in a local market. The brothers sell products directly to people in their city every day.

20. How do economists define market?

_____

_____

You can think of two types of markets as being necessary to produce goods and services in a market economy—a resource market and a product market. These markets involve resources, producers, and consumers. You learned in Chapter 1 that factors of production, or productive resources, are capital resources, human resources, and natural resources. **Producers** are people who create goods and services. Individuals, or **consumers**, are people who buy goods and services to satisfy their wants and needs.

TAKE ANOTHER LOOK

The flowcharts below show what happens both in a resource market and in a product market.

In a **resource market**, producers pay individuals for productive resources that they need to make products. In a **product market**, consumers pay money to producers for products.

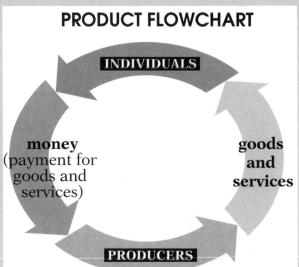

RESOURCE FLOWCHART

INDIVIDUALS

money (payment for factors of production)

factors of production (human, capital, natural)

PRODUCERS

PRODUCT FLOWCHART

INDIVIDUALS

money (payment for goods and services)

goods and services

PRODUCERS

21. What do individuals do in a product market?

_____

_____

22. What do producers do in a resource market?

_____

_____

23. In a resource market, who provides producers with factors of production?

_____

_____

The Economic System of the United States

The Wong family came from China to the United States for one reason—the U.S. economic system. As Geng said, "The economic system is much better here." In the U.S. economic system, government has some control over businesses, but it is limited. People have a voice in how to use resources within the limits of the law. The U.S. economic system has many features of a market economy. They are:

- economic freedom
- voluntary exchange of goods and services
- profit motive
- private property

Economic Freedom **Economic freedom** allows individuals to make economic decisions that they believe are in their own best interest. For example, economic freedom allowed Geng to make several decisions on his own. First, he decided to save money to open a store. Once Geng completed the necessary paperwork and opened the store, he decided what he wanted to sell; from whom he would buy the goods that he would sell; how he would market those goods; and what prices he would charge. A **price** is the amount of money asked or paid for something. At no time did the government tell Geng what he could or could not do about saving for, planning, opening, or running his own business.

24. Explain economic freedom.

_____

_____

_____

_____

25. What is price?

_____

_____

_____

Voluntary Exchange of Goods **Voluntary exchange** means that people trade freely with one another. Voluntary exchange occurs when sellers can sell their products at whatever price they choose and when buyers are free to either buy or refuse to buy the products.

For example, Geng can try to sell sunflowers for $1 apiece if he so chooses. A buyer can then decide whether he or she wants to buy sunflowers at that price. If the buyer agrees to buy a sunflower at $1, a voluntary exchange has taken place. Both people have agreed to the terms of the exchange.

26. What is voluntary exchange?

_____

_____

Profit Motive In a market economy, production is done by businesses and individuals in order to make a profit. **Profit** is the money made by a business after all costs have been paid. If a business' income is less than its costs, then it has sustained a **loss**.

For example, Geng buys goods from distributors to sell in his store. He must also pay other expenses, such as rent, electricity, and insurance. Geng's profit or loss is the difference between the amount of money that the store takes in and the total amount paid for expenses. Geng is always searching for the greatest profit. That search is called the **profit motive**. This motive is what drives people, such as Geng, to start and operate their own business.

27. What is profit?

_____

_____

28. What is the profit motive?

_____

_____

29. When does a loss occur?

_____

_____

Sometimes businesses don't manage to earn any profit. Businesses may break even or even lose money. In a market economy, businesses produce goods and services that business owners think people want to buy. Business owners try to produce and/or sell items that they can sell for more than their costs. This means the business will make a profit.

For example, Geng sells flowers at one of his stores. Geng buys the flowers from a distributor for $2 a dozen. He sells them at his store for $5 a dozen so that he makes a profit from selling the flowers.

Private Property In a market economy, most property is private property. **Private property** is property owned by individuals and businesses, rather than by the government. People have the right to buy, sell, and use their property in any way they want within the law.

30. What is private property?

_____

_____

Functions of U.S. Government in the Economy

The U.S. economic system is primarily a market economy. Most economic decisions are made by individuals. But the federal government has an important role. You will learn more about these functions as you read other chapters in this book. Following is a brief look at some of its most important roles.

Most importantly, the federal government protects private property rights. It is the responsibility of the U.S. government to protect individual property from being violated or taken away illegally by other individuals or by the government. The federal government also has created laws to protect competition. **Competition** exists when producers or sellers sell similar products. Competition also results in businesses offering the best products at the lowest prices and with the best service.

31. What is competition?

_____

_____

Another way that the U.S. government helps the economy is by trying to help with economic problems, such as inflation or unemployment. It does this in a number of ways, such as raising or lowering taxes or increasing or decreasing government spending. The central banking system can also increase or decrease the total amount of money available for lending in the economy. If the banks decrease the amount of available money to loan, the economy will slow down. If the banks increase the amount of available money to loan, the economy will speed up.

32. What are some ways that the U.S. government can help the economy?

_____

_____

_____

33. How does the federal government help the economy?

_____

_____

34. How do banks slow down the economy?

_____

_____

35. How do banks speed up the economy?

_____

_____

The federal government also provides many of the public facilities and services that its citizens need or want. These include providing a national defense, providing benefits and services to veterans, and running the national parks.

36. What is an important public service that the federal government provides?

_____

_____

✔Check Your Understanding

Check your understanding of the ways that the United States functions in the economy by filling in the chart below.

FUNCTIONS OF THE U.S. GOVERNMENT IN THE ECONOMY		
PROTECTS	PROVIDES	HELPS
_____	_____	_____
_____	_____	_____
_____	_____	_____
_____	_____	_____

Reading a Comparison Chart

A chart is another way to compare information quickly. The chart below shows the major differences between the economic systems of China and the United States. At a quick glance, you can see that the two economic systems are quite different.

CHINA'S ECONOMY *vs.* the U.S. ECONOMY

System Characteristic	China	United States
Type of economy	primarily command	primarily market
Business owned by	government	individuals & businesses
Level of economic freedom	generally low	very high
Prices set by	government	individuals & businesses
Source of income for individuals	wages, profit (very limited)	wages, profit, interest, rent, investments

Read the title and the column headings for each column to find out what information the chart shows. Then look at the column on the left. This column shows each characteristic that is being compared. To use the chart, read each system characteristic. Then move to the right to see what that characteristic is for China and the United States.

Use the chart to answer the following questions.

1. Which country has mostly a command economic system?

_____

2. Which country has mostly a market economic system?

_____

3. Who owns most of the businesses in China?

_____

4. Who owns most of the businesses in the United States?

_____

5. Which country has more economic freedom?

_____

6. In which country are prices set by the government?

_____

Vocabulary

Complete each sentence with a term from the list below.

market	producers
economic system	tradition-based economic system
market economic system	mixed economic system
command economic system	economic freedom
capitalism	voluntary exchange
consumers	

1. A central authority owns and controls the factors of production in a

_____ .

2. An economy that has characteristics of all three economic systems

is a _____ .

3. _____ occurs when sellers can sell products at whatever price they choose and when buyers are free to buy or refuse to buy the products.

4. _____ create goods and provide services.

5. An _____ is the way a society uses its resources to produce and distribute goods and services.

6. To an economist, a _____ refers to the actions of buying and selling.

7. A _____ leaves production and distribution decisions to individuals and businesses.

8. Production and distribution decisions are based largely on custom

in a _____ .

9. _____ are those who buy goods and services to satisfy their wants and needs.

10. _____, or free enterprise, is the same as a market economic system.

11. _____ allows people to make economic decisions that they think are in their own best interest.

Main Idea

Answer the following questions.

12. Suppose you just met a person from another country. How would you describe the U.S. economic system to that person?

_____

_____

13. How much competition is there among the stores in your community? For example, is there just one store or many stores that sell food? If there are many, how do you decide where to shop?

_____

_____

_____

Understanding Economics

14. Chuck wants to open a business. Identify the steps that Chuck might take to start his business. Describe how these steps illustrate the characteristics of economic freedom. Explain in economic terms what is probably going on.

_____

_____

_____

_____

_____

_____

Project

Do you know someone who has immigrated to the United States? Work as a class to interview this person about the economic system of the country from which he or she came. Write your interview questions beforehand. You can use what you have learned in this chapter as a guide. Then have a class discussion. Compare and contrast the economic system that you learn about with the U.S. economic system. You may want to make a comparison chart to summarize your findings.

It's Friday night. You're lacing up your Nike athletic shoes when you hear the doorbell. A delivery person stands in the doorway holding a steaming Domino's pizza. You pay for the pizza and give him a tip. As you watch the delivery person walk away, you notice that he's wearing Nikes, just like you.

How is it that, by the mid-1990s, names, such as Nike and Domino's, had become so familiar to so many people? Can wearing the right sneakers and eating the right pizza really make you cool? Or is it all just hype? More important, how did these companies become large and famous? Was there ever a time when people just wore plain old sneakers and ate plain old pizza?

A Tale of Two Companies

To find out, let's rewind to earlier times. Both Domino's and Nike started out small. In the early 1980s, most pizzerias like Domino's were locally owned. However as time passed, Domino's expanded. One Domino's soon became dozens. Dozens became hundreds. By the late 1980s, Domino's had become a nationwide giant.

Nike's path to success was different. Nike started out as a specialty company. It made running shoes primarily for serious long-distance runners. In 1974, Nike introduced its Waffle Trainer running shoes. They were stronger, lighter, and more comfortable than any others. They

How did Nike and Domino's do it?

performed better than old-fashioned sneakers. By the late 1970s, Nike led a running-shoe craze that swept the nation. By the mid-1980s, Nike was the leading athletic shoe company in the country.

The Secrets of Their Success

Many people credit Domino's success to just one thing: timeliness. Before Domino's, ordering a pizza for delivery could be a real adventure. Sometimes, it came in 20 minutes or it could take hours.

Domino's took advantage of that situation, and the company decided to use advertising to do it. Domino's created its famous 30-minute pledge: If your pizza didn't arrive in 30 minutes, you got it for free. People liked that idea, and each Domino's restaurant lived up to the

After becoming a nationwide giant, Domino's created its 30-minute pledge, which made Domino's one of the most successful pizza chains.

Nike took cool to new heights with its ads featuring soaring basketball star Michael Jordan.

guarantee. Rarely did it take longer than a half hour to deliver a Domino's pizza. When it did take longer, people got their pizza for free or received a large discount.

Nike, on the other hand, used high-quality products and endorsements from famous athletes to establish its reputation. Early on, Nike made the decision to sign up successful athletes to wear its shoes and appear in its ads. In the 1970s, Olympic runner Steve Prefontaine and tennis star John McEnroe became Nike athletes. In the

early 1980s, Olympic runner Joan Benoit joined the team. Then, in the mid-1980s, Nike signed up a young NBA Rookie of the Year named Michael Jordan—an athlete who would become one of basketball's biggest stars of all time.

Troubles

For a while, it seemed as if Nike and Domino's could do no wrong. If they were basketball teams, both had the equivalent of a 25-point lead in the fourth quarter. Then in 1989, a tragic traffic accident took place in Indiana. A 17-year-old driver was killed while delivering a Domino's pizza. Officials looked at the safety records of Domino's drivers. They found that many delivery vehicles had been in accidents. Soon, people began filing lawsuits against Domino's. They believed that the 30-minute pledge was causing delivery drivers to drive too fast and cause accidents.

Domino's fought back. The company denied that the 30-minute pledge was connected to unsafe driving. The bad publicity, however, proved to be too much. Domino's was forced to drop its 30-minute pledge. Domino's lost $300 million in sales between 1990 and 1992.

Nike's problems began when aerobic exercise became popular in the mid-1980s. As usual, Nike put out an excellent shoe for aerobic exercisers. It was well-designed and had superior performance. Compared to Reebok's sleek aerobics styles, however, Nike's aerobics shoes were bulky and clunky. Sales dropped. Profits plunged.

At the same time, Nike moved into casual, non-sports shoes. This was an even bigger disaster. By 1987, Nike sales had dropped by $200 million. Nike was forced to lay off 280 of its workers.

Both Nike and Domino's did a lot of

hard thinking. Management of both companies asked: Who are we? What are our strengths and weaknesses? What kind of advertising can get us back on top?

On the Rebound: Domino's

The answer for Domino's was to focus its advertising on teenagers. Pizza is the kind of food that fits a teenager's lifestyle. It's fun and fast to eat. It's not expensive. Polls showed, however, that teens didn't think eating Domino's pizza was cool.

In 1992, Domino's decided to come up with a new ad campaign. It would focus on the company's strengths: good ingredients, fast ("with safety in mind"), and free delivery. It would convince teens that eating Domino's was fun and fast—and cool!

By 1993, Domino's new image push was underway. Commercials featuring Donny Domino were aired on nationwide TV. Donny Domino was the company's cool cartoon character. The commercials were upbeat and fun. Domino's believed that the ads would persuade teenagers to buy Domino's pizza. Domino's said that the sales figures would tell whether the ads worked or not. If sales went up, then the ads were successful. If sales went down— well, Domino's hoped that the company wouldn't need to deal with that problem.

On the Rebound: Nike

Nike's path to recovery was also about image. "What was cool?" Nike asked. Ace basketball player Michael Jordan was cool. So Nike used him in an ad campaign for the Air Jordan basketball shoe. The ads show Jordan soaring through the air, looking like a mythical warrior. But cool was also a lot of other things. It was being a rebel, like tennis star Andre Agassi. It was being unpredictable, like basketball star Charles Barkley. It was being funny, like football/baseball star Bo Jackson. It

was not taking yourself too seriously, like Jordan's "Hare Jordan" ads with Bugs Bunny.

The Future

Sales figures in the past few years show Domino's creeping up slowly. In 1994, Domino's total sales hit $2.5 billion. The total was still more than $100 million below its 1990 peak, but it was well above Domino's 1992 low point.

For Nike, on the other hand, the sky seems to be the limit. Earnings were up about $1 billion for 1995. Nike's ads are universally admired. Its check-like symbol, the Nike swoosh, is instantly recognized. Polls show that among teens, Nike ranks third in name recognition, behind Disney and Universal Studios.

Domino's and Nike learned from experience. Both companies were able to regroup and come back. Today both are able to project an advertising image that convinces people to buy their products.

Domino's took aim at the teenage market with its ad campaign featuring cartoon character Donny Domino.

What Is Demand?

Whether these Domino's stores are successful depends, in part, on whether there is a demand for Domino's pizza in a particular marketplace. **Demand** is the amount of goods and services that people are willing and able to buy at different prices. For example, Rosie wants a pizza. She is willing to pay the price of a pizza, and she has enough money to pay for it. Rosie's desire is part of the demand for pizza. Three conditions create demand for goods:

- want or need

- willingness to pay

- ability to pay

All three conditions must be met for demand to exist. If Rosie would like to buy a jalapeño pizza, but she does not have enough money, then she would not be part of the demand.

1. What is demand?

_____

_____

2. When does demand for a product exist?

_____

_____

The Law of Demand

In most cases, the amount of a product that people buy depends on price. The **law of demand** states that as the price of a product decreases, people are willing to buy more—and as the price increases, people are willing to buy less. The table below shows how the law of demand works for jalapeño pizza.

Price of pizza	Number of pizzas people are willing to buy
$18	20
$16	40
$12	100
$10	200
$8	250

3. At what price was the quantity demanded for pizza lowest?

_____

4. At what price was the quantity demanded for pizza highest?

_____

5. What relationship do you see between price and amount of pizza people will buy?

_____

TAKE ANOTHER LOOK

The graph below shows the data from the table on page 41. The points on the graph represent the number of pizzas sold at each price. The points are connected by a smooth curve called a **demand curve**. It is easy to see that the number of pizzas people will buy increased as the price of the pizza decreased.

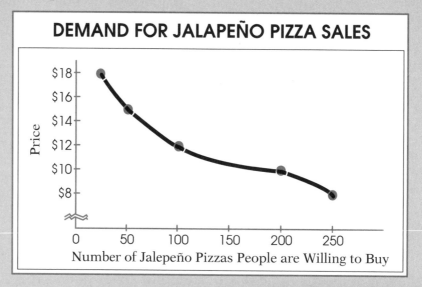

DEMAND FOR JALAPEÑO PIZZA SALES

6. As price decreases, how does the amount people are willing to buy change?

_____

7. As price increases, how does the amount people are willing to buy change?

_____

8. Explain how the graph supports the law of demand?

_____

Elastic and Inelastic Demand

The law of demand states that as you lower the price, the more of a good people are willing to buy. Lowering the price by a given amount, however, doesn't always result in the same change in the amount that people are willing to buy. For some goods, demand is elastic. **Elastic demand** occurs when a relatively small price change results in a relatively big change in the amount, or quantity, that people are willing to buy.

For example, imagine that Nike decreased the price of its sports sandals from $45 to $40. This price change increased sandal sales in one city from 300 pairs per week to 600 pairs per week. That large a change in the amount people bought for the change in price is an example of elastic demand.

However, there is not always a big change in the amount that people are willing to buy when a price is changed. This is called inelastic demand. **Inelastic demand** occurs when a change in price results in a relatively small change on the amount that people are willing to buy.

For example, imagine Nike dropped its price on Cross-Training shoes from $70 to $50. Now suppose that this decrease in price caused Cross-Training shoe sales in one city to go from 300 pairs in one week to 350 pairs. That small a change in the amount demanded in response to the price change is an example of inelastic demand.

9. What is elastic demand?

_____

_____

10. What is inelastic demand?

_____

_____

11. Give an example of elastic and inelastic demand from your own experience. Explain why you think each occurred?

_____

_____

_____

_____

✔ Check Your Understanding

Milk producers are well aware that demand for their product is inelastic. People will buy almost the same amount of milk whether the price increases or decreases. Pizza producers, on the other hand, know that the demand for their product is more elastic than the demand for milk. Far fewer people will buy an $18 pizza than a $15 pizza. Even at $15, some people might decide to skip the pizza and have hamburgers or gyros instead. Offer those same diners an $8 pizza, however, and they might just decide that they have a taste for pepperoni pizza.

12. Predict whether demand for bread would be elastic or inelastic. Support your answer.

_____

_____

13. Predict whether demand for tacos would be elastic or inelastic. Support your answer.

_____

_____

Changes in the Level of Demand

In 1989, Nike launched its "Just Do It" slogan with a commercial featuring athlete Bo Jackson. Jackson was playing the guitar with famous blues musician Bo Diddley. The level of demand for all styles of Nike's Bo Jackson shoes suddenly increased. People were not only willing to buy more shoes at higher prices, but they were also willing to buy shoes at lower prices. A change in demand occurs if people are willing to buy more or less of a product at different prices.

Changes in level of demand are influenced by many factors. Some of these factors are:

- what people's tastes are at any given time
- how much money people have to spend on a product
- how many people want a particular product
- how much money people expect to have in the future
- how much substitute products cost

Advertising plays a big role in changing the level of demand by trying to change people's tastes. As you learned earlier with Domino's and Nike, advertising can change people's preferences about products and influence their buying decisions. For example, many people agree that Nike has created an amazing advertising campaign for athletic shoes. To do this, Nike spent about 138 million advertising dollars to help raise the level of demand for athletic shoes. It worked! Sales increased tremendously.

14. Why do you think the level of demand for Bo Jackson shoes increased after the Bo Diddley and Bo Jackson ad appeared?

_____

_____

15. You read how the Donny Domino ad created an increased demand for Domino's Pizza. Which factors do you think most influenced the level of demand for Domino's Pizza? Explain your answer.

_____

_____

Competition

The Domino's in Porterfield had no competition last year. Remember, competition exists when a rivalry exists among producers or sellers who sell similar products. The table below shows how many large pepperoni pizzas were sold in Porterfield last year.

Name	Pizza	Price	Weekly sales
Domino's	Pepperoni	$10	500
Others	0	0	0

This year, a new pizza place called Pizza-Now moved into Porterfield. Pizza-Now is in competition with Domino's. Domino's no longer has the pizza market all to itself. The following table shows sales of the two pizza places.

Name	Pizza	Price	Weekly Sales
Domino's	Pepperoni	$10	300
Pizza-Now	Pepperoni	$10	200

16. How did competition from Pizza-Now affect Domino's sales?

_____

_____

A few months ago, Pizza-Now offered a special $8 pepperoni pizza. The table below shows pizza sales since Pizza-Now began its sale.

Name	Pizza	Price	Weekly Sales
Domino's	Pepperoni	$10	100
Pizza-Now	Pepperoni	$8	400

17. How did Pizza-Now's price change affect Domino's sales?

_____

Domino's soon offered an $8 pepperoni special of its own. Notice how sales changed when this happened.

Name	Pizza	Price	Weekly Sales
Domino's	Pepperoni	$8	325
Pizza-Now	Pepperoni	$8	375

18. What effect did competition have on Domino's prices?

_____

_____

19. Describe how the $8 price affected both competitors' sales.

_____

_____

Think About It!

In most cases, competition lowers prices for everyone. In the example above, Pizza-Now forced Domino's to lower its prices for pepperoni pizza. Had another pizza restaurant come to town, prices may have decreased even more.

Think of three companies with which you are familiar. Make a list of their products and their competitors.

	Company	Product	Competitor	Competitor
20.	_____	_____	_____	_____
21.	_____	_____	_____	_____
22.	_____	_____	_____	_____

Competition can lower prices only so much. Sellers generally aren't willing to sell products under what it costs them to produce the product.

What is Supply?

The law of demand says that the lower prices are, the more consumers are willing to buy. Buying and selling, however, is a two-way street. For every product, there is both a consumer and a producer. To fully understand prices, you need to look at both the consumer's and the producer's side of the situation.

In a market economy, consumers buy the goods that producers make, and producers make the goods that they think consumers will buy. **Supply** is how much producers are willing and able to sell at different prices. How do producers know how much of a good to make? They look at price. The **law of supply** states that as the prices of goods rise, producers will be willing to make more goods. As prices fall, producers will be willing to make fewer goods.

23. What is supply?

_____

_____

Producers are motivated by profit to make products. As you learned in Chapter 2, profit is the excess of the selling price over how much it costs to produce the product. For example, suppose the total cost for producing a pair of athletic shoes is $45. If those shoes sell for $55, the profit is $10:

Selling price − Costs = Profit

$55 − $45 = $10

If costs do not change, higher prices generally mean higher profits. According to the law of supply, when prices go up, producers are more willing to make more goods. Higher prices give producers the incentives to produce more goods when higher prices mean greater profits. The table below shows the relationship between prices and amount supplied for a special style of Nike hiking boots. As you can see, as the price decreases, the number of boots that Nike is willing to make also decreases.

Selling Price	Pairs of boots Nike is willing to make
$120	50,000
$100	20,000
$80	12,000
$60	8,000
$40	5,000

24. What is the law of supply?

_____

_____

25. Why are producers willing to make more goods when the price is high?

_____

_____

The graph below uses data from the table on page 47. The points on the graph represent pairs of boots that Nike was willing to make at each price. The points are connected by a smooth curve, called a **supply curve**. It is easy to see that as the price of the boots increases, the number of pairs of boots that Nike is willing to supply also increases.

SUPPLY OF HIKING BOOTS

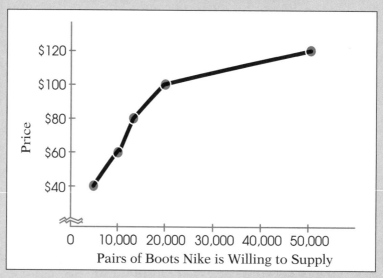

26. As price increases, how does the amount producers are willing to supply change?

_____

_____

27. Explain how the graph supports the law of supply.

_____

_____

Elastic and Inelastic Supply

Elastic supply is like elastic demand. You will recall that elastic demand occurs when a relatively small change in price results in a relatively large change in the amount that people are willing to buy. **Elastic supply** occurs when a relatively small change in price results in a relatively large change in the amount that producers are willing to supply.

You can see an example of elastic supply in Nike's hiking boot data. A price change from $100 to $120, resulted in a large change in the amount that Nike was willing to supply.

Similarly, inelastic supply works the same way as inelastic demand. **Inelastic supply** occurs when a price change results in a relatively small change in the amount that producers are willing to supply.

28. What is elastic supply?

_____

29. How is inelastic supply similar to inelastic demand?

_____

Costs

The amount a producer is willing to supply depends in part on costs. To make sneakers, for example, Nike has a whole range of costs. It has to pay for all of its productive resources, or factors of production. The company needs to pay for materials, wages, machinery, rent for buildings and factories, and advertising.

All of these expenses make up the production cost of a product. **Production cost** is the sum total of money that it takes to make a product. Low production cost may sometimes mean higher profits. High production cost may mean lower profits.

Production cost can be broken down into two types of costs: fixed costs and variable costs.

Fixed costs are the costs that a producer must pay to stay in business. Fixed costs stay the same no matter how much of a product the producer makes. Some of the costs of running a Nike factory remain the same whether the factory is producing 5,000 or 50,000 pairs of hiking boots a year. Fixed costs include:

- rent for buildings and factories
- purchase of machinery and equipment
- insurance

Variable costs are the costs that change as production increases or decreases. They include:

- raw material costs
- wages

Wages and raw material costs change when the amount of production changes. The Nike hiking boot factory will need many more workers and raw materials to produce 50,000 pairs of boots than it will to produce 5,000 pairs of boots. This means that variable costs will increase as production increases.

30. Why do companies try to keep production costs low?

_____

_____

31. What is the difference between fixed costs and variable costs?

_____

_____

Changes in the Level of Supply

Supply is the total amount of a product that producers are willing to produce at any one time at different prices. Some conditions cause producers to increase supply. Other conditions cause producers to decrease supply. Factors that can change the level of supply include:

- changes in production cost
- changes in technology
- changes in the number of competitors in the market

Changes in Production Cost For a company like Nike, the production cost can change for many different reasons. Cotton is a material used in making athletic shoes. A poor cotton harvest means higher prices for cotton and higher production cost for Nike. Increased production cost might decrease the total level of supply of athletic shoes. Other events could also influence the production cost. Workers could demand higher wages. Advertising rates could increase or decrease. Transportation costs could change. All these events could change the level of supply.

32. Think of an event that might change the production cost of pizza.

_____

33. Think of an event that might change the production cost of hiking boots.

_____

Changes in Technology A new computer program could help pizza makers schedule their deliveries more efficiently. Using technology would mean that workers could spend less time planning their deliveries and more time making pizzas. This increase in efficiency could lower the production cost of making pizza and could increase the level of supply for pizza.

Changes in Competition Suppose McDonald's were to enter the pizza market. Suddenly, Domino's would find itself with a major new competitor. This competition would increase the total supply of pizza on the market. Similarly, imagine what would happen if Pizza Hut, one of Domino's main competitors, were to go out of business. This would decrease the level of supply for pizza.

34. How do you think the supply of pizza would change if Burger King were to begin selling pizza?

_____

_____

Supply and Demand

The equilibrium price of a product represents a balance between supply and demand. The **equilibrium price** is the price at which the amount demanded equals the amount supplied. To see how an equilibrium price is found, look at the chart below.

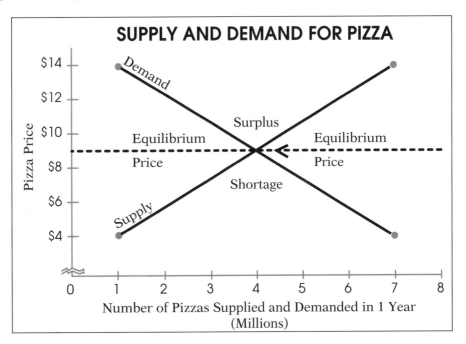

Looking at the graph, you can see that the equilibrium price occurs where supply and demand meet. The equilibrium price is $9

per pizza. At this price, producers supply 4 million pizzas a year, and consumers buy 4 million pizzas a year.

Suppose the market price for pizza were $6, which is $3 lower than the equilibrium price. At this low price, people would rush to buy pizza. Sellers would not be willing to supply as much pizza as consumers would want to buy. This would create a shortage. A **shortage** occurs when people want to buy more of a good than is available at a given price. A shortage puts pressure on prices to rise. Higher prices cause producers to increase the amount of pizzas supplied. Thus, a shortage tends to cause higher prices and increased production.

In an equilibrium situation, the pizza shortage above would cause pizza prices to rise to $9. In the real world, however, prices often overshoot or undershoot the equilibrium price. Suppose pizza prices rose to $11. Now, consumers start thinking pizza is too expensive. The quantity demanded falls. With far fewer people buying pizza, a surplus develops. A **surplus** occurs when there is too much of a good available at a given price. Pizza makers aren't selling as much pizza as they would like to sell. To sell more, they lower their prices. Therefore, a surplus puts pressure on prices and production to fall.

35. How does an equilibrium price come about?

_____

_____

_____

36. How does a market price below equilibrium create a shortage?

_____

_____

_____

37. What effect do shortages have on prices?

_____

_____

_____

38. What effect do surpluses have on prices?

_____

_____

_____

Reading a Supply and Demand Graph

The graph below shows a supply curve and a demand curve for Luckey's hot wings.

SUPPLY AND DEMAND FOR LUCKEY'S HOT WINGS

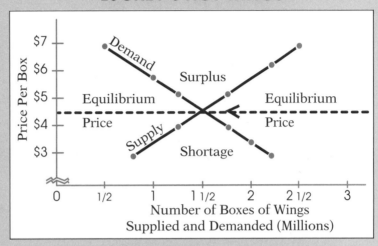

You can find out a lot of information from this graph. First, read the title and labels to see what information the graph shows. Look at the points on the supply curve and on the demand curve. Each supply curve point shows what producers are willing to supply at a given price. Each demand curve point shows what consumers are willing to buy at a given price.

The intersection point of the two curves shows the equilibrium price. You can also tell at which prices there would be a shortage of chicken wings and at which prices there would be a surplus.

Use the graph to answer the following questions.

1. What is the amount demanded for wings at $7 per box?

_____

2. What is the amount demanded for chicken wings at $6 a box?

_____

3. What is the equilibrium price for a box of chicken wings?

_____

4. At which prices would there be a shortage of chicken wings?

_____

5. At which prices would there be a surplus of chicken wings?

_____

Vocabulary

Complete each sentence with a term from the list below.

law of supply	elastic	fixed costs	law of demand
surplus	shortage	competition	inelastic

1. Costs that a producer must pay to stay in business are called

   _____.

2. A _____ occurs when there is too much of a good available at a given price.

3. _____ occurs when a rivalry exists among producers or sellers who sell similar products.

4. According to the _____, as prices of goods rise, producers will be willing to supply more goods.

5. A _____ occurs when there is not enough of a good available at a given price.

6. If supply is _____, the amount supplied will change a great deal as a result of a relatively small price change.

7. If supply is _____, the amount supplied will change very little as a result of a price change.

8. According to the _____, as the price of a product decreases, the more of a product people are willing to buy.

Main Idea

Answer the following questions.

9. How does price affect the amount producers are willing to supply? How does price affect the amount consumers are willing to buy?

   _____

   _____

10. How does competition affect prices?

   _____

   _____

11. How do supply and demand together lead to an equilibrium price?

_____

_____

_____

_____

Understanding Economics

12. Suppose you wanted to market an electric hat to keep people's heads warm. What would be included in your production cost?

_____

_____

_____

_____

13. Suppose you charged $20.00 for your hat. But at this price a big surplus exists. What would you do to sell the surplus hats?

_____

_____

_____

_____

14. Suppose you charged $5.00 for your hat. But at this price a big shortage exists. How would you get rid of the shortage?

_____

_____

_____

_____

Project

As a class, find how many students have athletic shoes. Then discuss what influenced your athletic-shoe buying decisions. Are you influenced by advertising? If so, which advertisements do you think were the most persuasive? Why? You may want to display the ads for discussion.

From salsa to rap, Vicky Perelli loves music. That's why she couldn't wait to work at the World Music Store. The day after the World Music Store opened, Vicky went straight to Mr. Martinez, the manager, and asked for a job. She told him how important music was to her and how much she knew about international musicians. Mr. Martinez asked Vicky if she was 18 years old and if she was still in school. Vicky told him that she was a senior in high school and wouldn't be 18 for three months.

Working on a Permit

Mr. Martinez told Vicky that he was sorry but he couldn't hire her unless she had working papers from the Board of Education in Philadelphia. He explained that in Pennsylvania people who are under the age of 18 and are still in school must have a work permit in order to be legally employed. Mr. Martinez also told Vicky that, even with a work permit, the state would only allow her to work 28 hours during the school week.

Vicky didn't want to deal with getting a work permit; it seemed like a hassle. So she decided to enjoy her last semester of school and wait until she was 18 to start work.

> ***Why does the government protect teenage workers?***

While she waited for her birthday and graduation, Vicky often wondered what the big fuss was about. She really loved music, knew a lot about it, and wanted to work at the music store. Why did the Pennsylvania government insist on work permits for people under the age of 18 who were still in school? What difference did it make whether she was 17 or 18 if she could do the job? Why couldn't she work more than 28 hours during the school week?

Before the U.S. Congress passed the 1938 Fair Labor Standards Act, many young children worked in factories for low pay and under dangerous conditions.

Learning from History

One day, Vicky learned why labor laws are so important. She had stopped by the store to remind Mr. Martinez that she would be turning 18 in a week. While they were talking, she decided to ask him why there were such strict laws about how old you had to be to work without a permit.

Mr. Martinez told Vicky that in the early 1900s there hadn't been any laws in the United States to protect children who worked. Many parents did not earn enough money to feed their children. These families could not afford for their children to be students and not workers. As a result, children were often hired to work in factories at very low wages. They earned a lot less than adults earned for doing the same jobs. The factories in which children worked were often dirty, poorly lighted, and dangerous. The children worked very long hours, as many as 14 each day, and never got the chance to go to school.

When Congress passed the Fair Labor Standards Act in 1938, it also enacted federal minimum wage laws.

As a result of these horrible conditions, the U.S. Congress passed the first federal child labor law in 1916 to protect children. The law set minimum age requirements for various types of work, and it called for an eight-hour work day and a 48-hour work week. In 1918, the U.S. Supreme Court ruled that law unconstitutional. For many years, people worked hard to get another labor law enacted. Twenty years later, the Fair Labor Standards Act of 1938 was passed. That law, later upheld by the U.S. Supreme Court, firmly established the constitutional legality of child labor laws.

In addition to the Fair Labor Standards Act of 1938, each state began to pass child labor laws that regulated the employment of children. The state laws established a minimum age for general employment and set limitations on daily and weekly hours. Today all 50 states have child labor laws, as do Puerto Rico and the District of Columbia. Federal and state laws vary. When there is a conflict between the federal law and a state law, the law that has a higher standard on behalf of the child applies.

Protecting People's Rights

When Congress passed the Fair Labor Standards Act in 1938, it also enacted federal minimum wage laws. These wage laws guaranteed that people would receive a certain amount of money an hour for their labor. In 1938, the minimum wage was set at 25 cents an hour. Since then, the minimum wage has been increased several times. The federal government increases the minimum wage by adding an amendment to the Fair Labor Standards Act. Since 1991, the federal minimum wage has been set at $4.25. All states must adhere to this minimum. Some states, however, chose to raise the minimum higher than $4.25. Nine states, including New Jersey, have opted for a higher minimum wage. In New Jersey, by state law, the minimum wage is $5.05.

By the time that Mr. Martinez had finished answering Vicky's question, she was speechless. She really couldn't believe that children in the United States had once been treated so poorly, had worked such long hours, and had been given no opportunity for an education. She finally understood why the government believed it was important to have laws that regulate the employment of young people.

A week later, Vicky was thinking of the minimum wage law as she rode the bus to her first day of work at the World Music Store. I finally have my dream job, Vicky thought. All day long, I can listen to salsa, rock, or flamenco and talk to people about music. At the same time, I will be working under good conditions and earning at least the minimum wage.

Understanding the labor laws that protect her, Vicky is happily employed at her dream job—a salesperson at a music store.

The U.S. Government's Role in the Economy

When Mr. Martinez told Vicky about the child labor laws, she learned that government plays a more important part in her life than she had realized. Vicky certainly hadn't known that she and other young people were protected by these child labor laws. She also didn't know that a law had been passed to make sure that employers pay a minimum wage. How else does government affect the U.S. economy?

The Biggest Employer in the U.S.

Government is, in fact, the biggest employer in the United States. The federal, state, and local governments in this country employ about 16 million workers, making government far and away the nation's largest employer. Government also takes in and spends more money than any business. This fact is one reason that government can, and does, have a huge impact on the U.S. economy.

1. What is one way that the government affects the U.S. economy?

_____

_____

_____

2. In what ways does the government protect young people? Use the case study to explain.

_____

_____

_____

_____

Levels of Government

There are three levels of government in the United States. They are:

- federal government
- state government
- local government

The highest level is the federal government. The center of the federal government is Washington, D.C., the capital of the United States. In addition to government at the federal level, each state, county, city, and town has its own government. There is an overlap in many services that the various levels of government provide. For example, protection of U.S. citizens is provided at the federal level by the U.S. Armed Forces, the FBI, and the CIA; at the state level by the National Guard and state troopers; and at the local level by municipal and county police officers.

3. What are the three levels of government?

_____

_____

4. What is the highest level of government?

_____

Economic Functions of Government

In Chapter 2 you read a little about the functions of the U.S. government in the economy. The economic functions of government may be divided into four categories. They are:

- providing public facilities and services
- providing public well-being
- regulating economic activity
- ensuring economic stability

Public Facilities and Services

One of the functions of government is to provide public facilities and services to its citizens. **Public facilities and services** include national defense, education, and some health care. For example, Vicky attends school in Philadelphia. Funding for her school's books, lunches, and education programs comes from federal, state, and local governments.

5. What are the four economic functions of government?

_____

_____

_____

_____

Other public services that the three levels of government provide are police and fire protection, public transportation, highways and bridges, and some hospitals. Federal, state, and local governments are all involved in providing these services. One public service provided only by the federal government is national defense. This service was one of the earliest ones that the federal government provided to its citizens. It is still a major function of the U.S. government today.

6. Name three public services provided by federal, state, and local governments.

_____

_____

_____

7. What service is provided only by the federal government?

_____

Public Well-Being

Another function of government is to provide for the general welfare of its citizens. The **general welfare** is the well-being of all citizens. Throughout much of the 20th century, the U.S. government has tried to guarantee a minimum level of economic well-being for all its citizens, especially those people who are most needy. In order to pay for their services to their citizens, governments collect taxes. **Taxes** are monies that governments collect from individuals and businesses.

For example, each week a certain amount of money will be deducted from Vicky's paycheck. The deductions include federal taxes, state taxes, and, in some places, city taxes. There is also a Social Security deduction. People pay a percentage of their salaries into the Social Security system and the Medicare system every year that they are employed. Employers also contribute to these systems on behalf of their employees. These taxes provide benefits, such as Social Security retirement, disability, and aid to minors whose parents have died.

8. What is the general welfare and how is it provided?

_____

_____

9. What are some deductions taken out of most paychecks?

_____

_____

By collecting taxes, governments are able to help people who are disabled or needy. The federal government spends about 40 percent of the money that it earns in taxes—almost $500 billion a year—to help people who are in economic difficulty. Medicare provides low-cost health care for the retired and the disabled. Workers' compensation provides payments to workers who have been injured on the job. These programs are supported by taxes.

10. Explain how government helps people who are disabled or needy.

_____

_____

Regulating Economic Activity

Another function of government is to regulate economic activity by:

- ensuring competition
- supervising working conditions
- protecting consumers
- protecting the environment

Ensuring Competition In Chapter 2 you learned that an important function of government is to protect private property rights. In so doing, it helps to promote competition among businesses. The federal government passes laws to protect competition and monitors the marketplace to make sure that it is competitive.

11. How does the federal government try to ensure that the marketplace remains competitive?

_____

Supervising Working Conditions The federal government also supervises working conditions. For example, you learned in this case study that the federal government established certain standards in the workplace when Congress passed the Fair Labor Standards Act of 1938. You also learned that the federal government established a minimum wage. Additionally, Congress passed laws making racial and gender discrimination illegal. It also passed the Equal Pay Act in 1963, which guarantees equal pay to men and women who do the same work. In 1970, Congress passed the Occupational Health and Safety Act. This act ensures that certain health and safety standards are followed in the workplace.

12. Name two laws that the federal government passed to supervise working conditions.

_____

_____

13. Which law did Congress pass to ensure equal pay for men and women working at the same type of job?

_____

_____

Protecting Consumers The federal government has passed laws to safeguard consumers against unfair marketing practices. For example, the Federal Trade Commission oversees the proper labeling of all products. The Food and Drug Administration tries to make sure that foods and drugs that are sold are safe. The federal government also protects consumers against **fraud**—people lying about themselves or a product to make a profit. One way that the federal government protects against fraud is through the U.S. Postal Service. The U.S. Postal Service has an inspection service. This service protects consumers from mail fraud.

For example, Mr. Martinez asks Vicky to order a particular CD of Brazilian music from a distributor. The advertisement states that the CD features several compositions by the late Milton Nascimento. When Vicky receives the CD, none of Nascimento's compositions are on it. Because Vicky ordered the CD through the mail, she can make a complaint to the U.S. Postal Inspection Bureau. This bureau will then investigate her complaint.

14. Name three ways that the federal government protects consumers?

_____

_____

_____

Protecting the Environment The federal government also protects the environment. In 1971, the federal government established the Environmental Protection Agency (EPA). This agency ensures that businesses meet clean air and water standards. If companies pollute, they must pay large fines.

15. Which federal government agency protects clean air and water standards?

_____

_____

Ensuring Economic Stability

The federal government also tries to ensure economic stability. It tries to keep the economy healthy. Economists are particularly concerned with two economic problems that can occur: unemployment and inflation.

To economists, **unemployment** occurs when people are willing and able to work but can't find jobs. **Inflation** is a sustained increase in the average level of prices in the whole economy. We will take a closer look at unemployment and inflation later in this chapter.

TAKE ANOTHER LOOK

Look at the table below. Read the title and the categories. Then answer the questions that follow.

ECONOMIC FUNCTIONS OF THE GOVERNMENT	
Public Facilities and Services	education, police, fire, public transport highways, bridges, national defense
General Welfare	Social Security, medicare, Aid to Families with Dependent Children, workers' compensation
Regulating Economic Activity	ensures competition, supervises working conditions, protects consumers, protects environment
Ensuring Economic Stability	tries to keep economy stable; monitors unemployment and inflation

16. What are four major economic functions of the U.S. government?

_____

_____

_____

_____

17. How does the federal government try to protect the environment?

_____

_____

Taxes: Paying for Government

As you have learned, government provides many services to its citizens. How does it pay for them? Mostly from taxes. Remember, taxes are monies that governments collect from individuals and

Read the paragraph below and answer the question that follows.

After working at the World Music Store for about a year, Vicky becomes friends with a co-worker named Jered. Jered and Vicky do the same type of work. She and Jered often go down the street for tacos or burritos at lunch. Yesterday, Jered told Vicky that he had received a raise last week. He's now making $6.50 an hour. Vicky was shocked to learn that she makes less than Jered even though they both do the same job, work the same number of hours, and received exactly the same job evaluation score. She decides to talk with Mr. Martinez about it.

18. What equal employment law might Vicky mention when talking with Mr. Martinez about her wages? Why?

_____

_____

_____

businesses. These monies help to support government programs. There are several kinds of taxes.

Income Taxes

Almost one-half of the money that the federal government takes in comes from **income taxes**. All people who work in the United States who earn more than a certain amount of money are legally obligated to pay a certain percentage of their earnings to the federal, state, and some city governments. This percentage depends on how much a person earns. Generally, the more a person earns, the higher the percentage, or tax rate. For example, Vicky probably pays less than 10 percent of her income in federal income tax. Mr. Martinez, who earns much more than Vicky, pays about 25 percent of his income in federal income tax. The personal income tax is a progressive tax. A **progressive tax** takes a higher percentage of earnings from those with higher income.

19. Why does Vicky pay less income tax than Mr. Martinez?

_____

_____

20. What is a progressive tax?

_____

_____

Workers in the United States also pay Social Security tax. This tax rate is about 7.65 percent of income. But workers pay this tax only on the first $62,700 or so of their income. Any yearly income over that amount is not taxed for Social Security. People who earn more than $62,700 end up paying a lower percentage of their total earnings in Social Security tax. Social Security is a regressive tax. A **regressive tax** takes a higher percentage of earnings from those with lower income.

21. What is a regressive tax?

_____

_____

Corporate Taxes

Corporate taxes account for a relatively smaller portion of the federal government's income. Corporations are obligated to pay a certain percentage of their profits to the federal government. The amount of the tax is based on how much the corporation earns. The federal government decides what the percentage will be. For example, World Music Store made a profit of $100,000 in 1995. The government decided that corporations making a profit of $100,000 would pay 34 percent of that profit in corporate taxes.

22. On what are corporate taxes based?

_____

_____

Excise Taxes

People in the United States pay federal excise taxes. **Excise taxes** are taxes on such items as gasoline and tobacco. Excise taxes are **indirect taxes** because the tax is on items bought, not on earnings of individuals. Income taxes and Social Security taxes are direct taxes. **Direct taxes** are taken out directly from the earnings of individuals.

23. Why are excise taxes indirect taxes?

_____

_____

24. What is the difference between an indirect tax and a direct tax?

_____

_____

_____

Tariffs

The federal government also taxes goods that are imported, or bought from other countries and brought into the United States. This tax is called a **tariff**. For example, Mr. Martinez sells music from around the world. In order to do that, he must import CDs and tapes from other countries and pay tariffs on them.

25. What is a tariff?

_____

_____

TAKE ANOTHER LOOK

ESTIMATED FEDERAL TAX RECEIPTS FOR 1996
(in billions of dollars)

Individual Income tax	$628.00
Corporate Income tax	$146.00
Social insurance (Social Security)	$518.00
Excise Taxes	$71.00
All other Taxes	$64.00
TOTAL	**$1,427.00**

26. From which group does the U.S. government collect the most taxes?

_____

_____

27. Which two taxes total more than the individual income tax?

_____

_____

The State of the Economy

Remember that the federal government works to ensure economic stability. When there are economic problems, the federal government may act to try to fix them. To do this, the federal government must keep a close watch on the economy. It looks at various indicators to see if the economy is performing well or poorly.

To find out how the economy is doing, the federal government looks at the Gross Domestic Product, or GDP. The **Gross Domestic Product** is a basic measure of how much an economy produces. Economists add up the values of all the final goods and services produced in a country during a year. The total is the GDP for that year. Economists use only the values of final goods and services to calculate the GDP. They don't add the values of goods and services that go into a product along the way. For example, economists do add the value of a new CD. They don't, however, add the values of the work, plastic, paper, and studio time that went into making the CD. The values of all of these goods are part of the value of the final product.

28. What is one measure that the federal government looks at to find out how the economy is doing?

_____

_____

29. How is the GDP calculated?

_____

_____

GDP and the Business Cycle

The Gross Domestic Product, or GDP, is a measure of the size of an economy. When the GDP increases from year to year, this indicates that the economy is growing. Over the past 50 years or so, the U.S. economy has grown enormously. Not every year, however, is a good economic year. In some years, the economy has a growth spurt. In other years, it grows very little. There are still other years when the GDP decreases. During these years, fewer goods and services are produced than during prior years—resulting in unemployment.

This pattern of change in the economy is called the business cycle. The **business cycle** is the cycle of alternating strong and weak periods in the economy. A period of economic growth is usually followed by a period of economic slowdown. The government tries to strengthen the economy when it's weak. It also tries to slow down inflation.

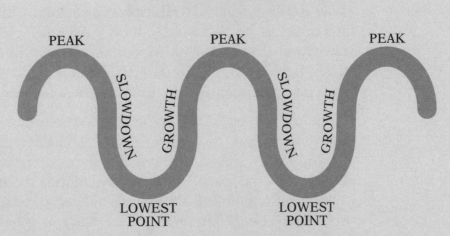

THE BUSINESS CYCLE

TAKE ANOTHER LOOK

PEAK PEAK PEAK

SLOWDOWN GROWTH SLOWDOWN GROWTH

LOWEST POINT LOWEST POINT

30. In which period of the business cycle is the economy really strong?

_____

31. How does the business cycle model show strength in the economy?

_____

32. How does the business cycle model show weakness in the economy?

_____

Unemployment and Economic Stability

As stated earlier, unemployment occurs when people are willing and able to work but can't find jobs. Often, a weak economy will increase the number of unemployed people. Also, some unemployment is seasonal. For example, construction workers in northern states may be unemployed during the winter months because it is too cold to work outside. Most economists believe that the economy will always have some unemployment.

33. How do economists define unemployment?

_____

_____

34. What effect does a weak economy often have on the number of unemployed people?

_____

_____

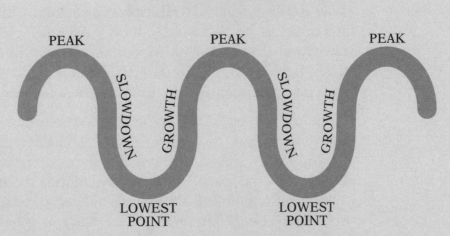

Inflation, Deflation, and Economic Stability

As stated earlier, inflation is a sustained rise in the average level of prices in the economy. **Deflation** is a sustained fall in the average level of prices in the whole economy. Average price levels may rise slowly over time in a healthy economy. When this rise is slow and steady, people are prepared for it. When it becomes rapid, though, or when prices suddenly drop, lives and businesses can be disrupted.

Inflation can occur when the demand for goods and services grows faster than the supply of goods and services. Increased demand makes supplies scarce and drives up prices. This is described by the law of supply and demand, about which you learned in Chapter 3. Inflation can also occur when the costs of production rise. When production costs rise, businesses may raise their prices to cover their costs.

One way changes in price levels are recorded is by the Consumer Price Index. The **Consumer Price Index** compares average prices of selected goods and services in one year with those of an earlier, or base, year.

35. What is inflation?

_____

36. What is deflation?

_____

Unemployment and inflation are two problems that concern economists. Look at the chart that follows. For each problem, write two situations that economists think cause it.

┌───┐
| SOME ECONOMIC PROBLEMS |
| UNEMPLOYMENT   INFLATION |
| |
| _____   _____ |
| |
| _____   _____ |
└───┘

Reading a Circle Graph

A pie graph can help you see how a whole is broken into parts. The pie graph below shows the taxes that the federal government estimates it will collect in 1996. Looking at it, you can quickly compare the size of the "slices." You can also quickly see the types of federal taxes that will be collected.

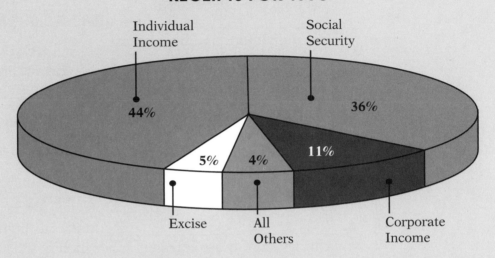

ESTIMATED FEDERAL TAX RECEIPTS FOR 1996

Individual Income — 44%
Social Security — 36%
Excise — 5%
All Others — 4%
Corporate Income — 11%

Read the title of the graph and the labels to see what information is on the graph. The labels tell you the various types of taxes that are collected. Each slice of the pie graph shows a percentage of the total taxes that the federal government estimates it will collect in 1996. The whole pie represents 100 percent of the total taxes that the federal government expects to collect.

1. Which tax accounts for the greatest share of tax monies that the federal government estimates it will collect in 1996?

_____

2. What percentage of the total federal tax receipts does the federal government estimate that corporate taxes will account for in 1996?

_____

3. Which type of tax does the federal government think will account for about 4 percent of the total taxes collected in 1996?

_____

Vocabulary

Complete each sentence with a term from the list below.

taxes	regressive taxes	progressive taxes
deflation	corporate taxes	Gross Domestic Product
inflation	direct taxes	Consumer Price Index

1. _____ are monies that governments collect from individuals and businesses.

2. _____ take a higher percentage of earnings from those earning lower incomes.

3. _____ are paid by corporations.

4. _____ is a sustained increase in the average level of prices in the whole economy.

5. Income taxes and Social Security taxes are _____.

6. _____ take a higher percentage of earnings from those earning higher incomes.

7. _____ is a sustained decrease in the average level of prices in the whole economy.

8. The _____ is the total value of all the final goods and services produced in a country during a year.

9. The _____ compares average prices of selected goods and services in one year with those of an earlier, or base, year.

Main Idea

10. What are some of the roles that the U.S. government plays in the economy?

_____

_____

_____

_____

_____

11. How does the government pay for some of the goods and services that it provides?

_____

_____

Understanding Economics

12. Suppose that you have a full-time job at a local clothing store. How might government involvement in the economy affect your life? What taxes might you pay? From which services might you benefit?

_____

_____

13. Choose a public service that you and your classmates use. Write a one-paragraph letter to the editor of a local newspaper explaining why this service is valuable to the community and needs to continue being provided.

_____

_____

_____

_____

_____

_____

_____

_____

_____

Project

What public services operate in your community? Research the range of services provided by the local, state, and federal governments. As a class, choose one of these services. Then investigate what this service offers. What does it provide? To whom does it provide the service? Is the service useful? What do the people who use the service think about it? Use a separate sheet of paper to write a report of your findings.

In 1995, *Rolling Stone* magazine named the Schwinn Classic Cruiser its "hot" vehicle of the year. How did an old 1-speed bicycle from the 1950s get to be so popular in the mid 1990s? It's just one piece of a long story—the story of the Schwinn Bicycle Company of Boulder, Colorado.

The Road to Success

In 1995, Schwinn celebrated its 100th birthday. German immigrant Ignaz Schwinn founded the company in Chicago in 1895. Schwinn and his partner, Adolph Arnold, picked a good time to start a bicycle company. A lot of Americans had begun to ride bicycles. Schwinn and Arnold considered the bicycle a viable replacement for the horse. It was relatively cheap and fairly easy to make. More importantly, a bicycle—unlike a horse—needs no feeding and little care.

The bicycle boom didn't last long. After the turn of the century, a new vehicle suddenly appeared on the scene—the gasoline-powered car. The introduction of cars nearly wiped out the bicycle market. All but a few of the

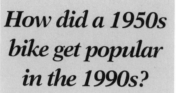

How did a 1950s bike get popular in the 1990s?

country's five hundred bicycle companies closed down for good.

The Schwinn company was one of the few survivors. It survived because it had a new strategy. No longer would Schwinn focus on selling bicycles to adults. Instead, it would focus on children. They were the bicycle riders of the future.

Schwinn's success grew as a result of this marketing change. Also, its reputation for quality was unmatched. Schwinn bicycles were strong, solid, and dependable. Schwinn was also a leader in innovation. In the 1930s and 1940s, Schwinn introduced

At the turn of the century, the bicycle became a replacement for the horse.

By the late 1960s, the children of the 1940s were parents buying bicycles for their own children.

such new devices as the built-in bicycle lock, the saddle seat, front-wheel brakes, fender reflectors, and the fender headlight.

Generations of children grew up with Schwinn bikes. In the 1940s, Schwinn ads featured Hollywood stars, such as Frank Sinatra. By the late 1960s, the children of the 1940s were parents buying bicycles for their own kids. The brand they chose most often was Schwinn.

Moving Ahead

In the 1960s and early 1970s, Schwinn was still riding high. It replaced its Classic Cruisers and Black Phantoms with new models. Schwinn Sting Rays, with their "banana" seats, were a major hit of the 1960s. To capture the racer market, Schwinn introduced the 10-speed Varsity. The Schwinn Orange Krate, Apple Krate, and Manta Ray models were just as successful as the models before them. Up until the mid-1970s, Schwinn was still the leader in bicycle sales. In good years, it held as much as 25 percent of the bicycle market.

Then, in the late 1970s and early 1980s, the bicycle market began to change. First, companies like Huffy and Murray began making inexpensive models for young children. At the same time, mountain bikes became popular for older riders.

Instead of fighting these new challenges, Schwinn rested on its past glories. When asked about their competition, Schwinn officials scoffed. "We don't have competition," they said. "We're Schwinn." This attitude soon created problems. By the early 1980s, Schwinn's market share began to shrink. Meanwhile, mountain-bike sales kept rising through the 1980s and 1990s. Schwinn officials kept insisting that mountain bikes were simply a fad.

By 1992, over two-thirds of all bicycles sold in the United States were mountain bikes. Suddenly, Schwinn was in real trouble. Its market share had shrunk to a fraction of its level in the 1960s and 1970s. As late as 1987, Schwinn sold one million bikes in the United States per year. In the early 1990s, Schwinn was selling fewer than 300,000 bikes per year.

Collapse

In 1992, the unthinkable happened. Schwinn, once the giant of the bicycle industry, went bankrupt. The family-owned company could not make the payments on its loans. For a while, it appeared that the Schwinn name might

By 1992, over two-thirds of all bicycles sold in the United States were mountain bikes.

Schwinn was still the most recognizable brand in the bicycle industry. But its reputation had suffered. People thought Schwinns were heavy and clunky. "When I was a kid, if you had a Schwinn, you were the luckiest kid in the world," said bicycle executive Scott Montgomery in the early 1990s. "Ask a college kid now, and they'll say, 'Oh Schwinn? They're toast.'"

The Comeback Begins

To build Schwinn back up, Zell handed the company over to former Olympic skier Chuck Ferries. Ferries became chairman of the company's board of directors. He and Chief Executive Officer Tom Stendahl took immediate and drastic action. First, they moved the company headquarters from Chicago, Illinois, to Boulder, Colorado. Boulder is the center of one of the country's largest mountain-biking communities.

The two Schwinn executives then cut Schwinn's work force down from 300 workers to 180. They also hired a new type of worker. The "old" Schwinn workers wore shirts and ties. The new Colorado workers were T-shirt-wearing mountain bikers. Instead of driving cars to work, they rode their bikes. Instead of playing golf on weekends, they headed for the mountain-biking trails. Ferries hoped that their enthusiasm would breathe new energy into the company.

disappear. Then multimillionaire Sam Zell came on the scene. Zell specialized in buying companies that had lost their way. He purchased Schwinn for $43 million. For the first time ever, the Chicago-based company was not controlled by family members. "It's as classic a business tragedy as you're going to find anywhere," said one industry expert.

Zell knew that the Schwinn name was still worth something. Among baby boomers, people born after 1945,

The Plan

After the 1994 reorganization, Ferries changed the entire Schwinn product line. "The key to getting Schwinn back was the product redesign," Ferries said. "Schwinn was not making a top-quality mountain bike."

Ferries set his young designers to work revamping Schwinn's line of mountain bikes. Their experience on the bike trails helped them to design sleek new models. Before long, Schwinn's factories were turning out bicycles that were unlike any that Schwinn had produced before.

But were they good enough? Were they different enough? Were people ready to plunk down $350 or more for a high-tech bicycle bearing the Schwinn name? Many Schwinn dealers were doubtful. In 1993, Ferries sent Schwinn sales representatives to more than 800 Schwinn dealers across the United States. Their mission was to convince the dealers that Schwinn was truly back. Its products were better. Its new attitude was contemporary. It could compete with the leaders in the mountain-bike market, including Trek, Cannondale, and others. Asked if Schwinn could return to its former level of success, dealer Michael W. Koch replied, "Chrysler did it, didn't they?"

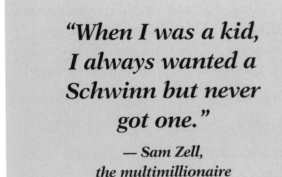

> "When I was a kid, I always wanted a Schwinn but never got one."
>
> — Sam Zell,
> the multimillionaire
> who bought Schwinn

In 1994, Schwinn designers began revamping Schwinn's line of mountain bikes.

Competition and Market Structure

Suppose you want to start your own bicycle business. Rather than make new bicycles, you decide to rebuild classic bicycles and sell them. One thing that you would need to do is find out whether demand exists for classic bicycles. In fact, Schwinn Black Phantom bicycles from the 1950s now sell for as much as $7,000. This high price convinces you that your business might be a good idea.

To get started, you will need:

- a location—a shop
- equipment—tools, supplies, parts
- materials—old Black Phantom bicycle frames

Next, you give your business a name: Classic Bicycles. To run your business, some of the things that you need to do are:

- advertise—to help customers find out about your business
- keep records—to keep track of money that you spend and money that you take in
- hire employees—to help you with the work

1. What is one thing that you need to start a business?

_____

2. What is one thing that you need to run a business?

_____

Capital and Interest

Another BIG thing that you need to start a business is money. The financial costs of running your business are examples of **expenses**. Your business expenses would include buying supplies, paying rent, paying your workers, buying old bicycles, and advertising.

Money that you use to start a business is an example of **financial capital**. To pay start-up costs and expenses, businesses need large amounts of financial capital. In some cases, people use their own money as capital for a business. Most of the time, however, business owners borrow capital from banks or investors. **Investors** are people who put money into something, such as stocks, real estate, or a business, in order to make a profit in the future.

In the case of your bicycle business, suppose that you get a $20,000 loan from a bank. Why would a bank be willing to lend you $20,000? It would if your business seems to be a good risk and you promise to pay the loan back with interest. **Interest** is the extra amount of money that you pay for the privilege of using others' money. Interest is calculated as a percentage of the amount that you borrow. Over time, you may have to pay a total of $25,000 to pay off your $20,000 loan. Five thousand of that $25,000 is the interest that the bank charges you for the use of its money.

3. What are expenses?

_____

4. What is financial capital?

_____

5. What is interest?

_____

Types of Business Structures

How will you organize Classic Bicycles? You might decide to become the sole proprietor of the business. A **sole proprietor** is a person who owns and runs a business by himself or herself. A sole proprietor makes all decisions and keeps all profits from a business, but is also responsible for any losses.

To share some of that responsibility, people often get a business partner. A business owned by two or more people is called a **partnership**. In a **general partnership**, partners make decisions together. They also share both profits and losses. General partners will both lose their assets if their business has problems. In a **limited partnership**, the limited partner often does not make decisions. The limited partner is often responsible only for the amount of money that he or she has invested in the business. If the business fails, the limited partner will sometimes lose only the amount of money invested.

A third type of business is called a corporation. A **corporation** is a business that is owned by its stockholders. Each share of stock represents ownership in a corporation. **Stockholders** are people who own shares of stocks in and own a corporation. Some stockholders elect the members of the corporation's board of directors and decide corporate policies by voting. Stockholders may share in some of the profits of a corporation, but they are not responsible for any losses. However, if a corporation does not do well, its stockholders lose money by not getting dividends and by their stocks' value going down.

Only about 20 percent of all businesses in the United States are corporations, but all of the big U.S. businesses are corporations. Most small businesses are sole proprietorships. They make up about 70 percent of the businesses in the United States. Partnerships make up about 10 percent of the businesses in the United States.

6. What is a sole proprietorship?

_____

7. What is a partnership?

_____

8. What is a corporation?

_____

_____

Running a Corporation

If you wanted to turn Classic Bicycles into a corporation, you would first need to get a charter. One type of **charter** is a state license that allows you to do business as a corporation. This charter can cost anywhere from a few hundred to a few thousand dollars.

A corporation is treated much like a person in the eyes of the law. Corporations can make contracts, hire workers, own property, and borrow money. A corporation can also sue or be sued in court.

What is the advantage of becoming a corporation? Suppose your business does not do well. As a sole proprietor or a general partner in a business, you risk losing your personal money and possessions. **Risk** refers to the chance of losing something valuable.

For example, let's say the producers from whom you bought your goods want to be paid, but your business does not have enough money. These producers could decide to sue for the money that they are owed. If you are not incorporated, people can sue you directly as the business owner. In some cases, they can even take your savings, house, and other assets. As a stockholder in a corporation, you risk only the money that you invested in the corporation. People cannot sue you directly as the owner of the business. They can only sue the corporation and take away the corporation's property.

9. What is one type of charter?

_____

_____

10. What advantage do corporations have over sole proprietorships?

_____

_____

Let's look at another way of comparing sole proprietorships, partnerships, and corporations. The table below shows ways that they are similar and ways that they differ. Read the table and answer the questions that follow.

COMPARISON OF BUSINESS STRUCTURES

	SOLE PROPRIETORSHIP	GENERAL PARTNERSHIP	CORPORATION
Easy to organize?	yes	somewhat	no
Who is responsible for success?	proprietor	partners	corporate leaders
Who makes decisions?	proprietor	Partners must agree.	corporate leaders and stockholders
Who takes risks?	Proprietor risks everything.	Partners share risk.	Stockholders risk their investments only.
Who gets profits?	proprietor	shared among partners	part may go to stockholders; rest may be reinvested in corporation
Who takes losses?	proprietor	shared among partners	corporation

11. Which business structure seems most risky for an individual?

_____

12. In which business structure do a few people share profits and losses?

_____

13. If you were going to start a business, which business structure would you be most interested in starting? Explain why.

_____

_____

_____

_____

_____

Organization of a Corporation

The stockholders of a corporation are the owners of the corporation, but they don't run it. Some stockholders can elect the board of directors. Some can also vote on important issues facing the corporation. The **board of directors** makes the most important decisions about the corporation. It sets goals and decides policies. It also determines how profits will be divided.

To run the company on a day-to-day basis, the board of directors hires a chief executive officer, or CEO. The **chief executive officer** is responsible for carrying out the decisions of the board of directors. Some corporations have presidents as well as CEOs. The chart below shows an example of how a corporation might be organized.

Corporate Organization

STOCKHOLDERS
- own the corporation
- provide investment capital
- sometimes elect a board of directors
- sometimes vote on issues

BOARD OF DIRECTORS
- makes decisions about goals and policies
- chooses a CEO and other corporate officers

CEO (and other corporate officers)
- carries out decisions made by the board of directors
- heads all corporation divisions

VICE-PRESIDENTS
- head individual divisions
- report to the CEO

DEPARTMENT HEADS
- head individual departments
- report to the vice-presidents

EMPLOYEES
- carry out the work of the company
- report to department heads

A large corporation may be organized so that people oversee each other's work. The department heads oversee employees. Vice-presidents oversee department heads. The CEO and other corporate officers oversee vice-presidents. The board of directors oversees the CEO and the other corporate officers. In the end, the board of directors is responsible for whatever the corporation does. If the stockholders aren't pleased, then they can elect new directors.

14. Overall, who is responsible for what a corporation does?

_____

_____

15. What are the responsibilities of the CEO?

_____

_____

16. Suppose an employee of a corporation does especially good work. How might the CEO get word of this good work?

_____

_____

How Corporations Raise Capital

One way for businesses to raise money is to borrow it. A proprietor or partnership might borrow money from friends, family, a bank, or a government loan program.

Corporations raise money from investors by issuing stocks and bonds. You will learn more about investing in stocks and bonds in Chapter 8. A **bond** is an interest-bearing certificate issued by a corporation or the federal government that can be cashed in by a specific date. When a bond is issued, the corporation promises to pay a certain amount of interest over a certain amount of time on the money that it borrowed and agrees to repay the amount borrowed on a certain date.

A **stock** is a share of ownership in a corporation. People who buy stock in a company are called stockholders. Each unit of stock is called a **share**. The more shares that a stockholder has, the larger the part of the corporation he or she owns. Common stockholders get one vote in corporate elections for each share of stock that they own. Preferred stockholders have no voting rights.

Stockholders may receive a small part of the corporation's profits in the form of dividends. A **dividend** is the portion of a corporation's profits that is distributed among its stockholders. In most cases, however, stockholders make most of their profit by selling their stocks for more money than they paid for them. For example, suppose that you bought 20 shares of stock at $40 a share for a total of $800. If you sold that stock when it was selling for $80 a share, then you would receive $1,600. Subtract your original investment of $800, and you have a profit, or capital gain, of $800.

17. How do corporations raise capital?

_____

_____

18. What are the two ways that stockholders can make money?

_____

_____

_____

Free Markets and Competition

Schwinn has begun producing brand-new Classic Cruisers in its factories. You have decided that you will sell these Classic Cruisers at your Classic Bicycles shop. What selling price will you ask for the Classic Cruisers?

If perfect competition existed, the selling price would be freely determined by many buyers and sellers. **Perfect competition** means that no one buyer or seller has control over the price of a good.

Perfect competition exists if:

- All sellers offer the same product.
- All sellers and buyers are free to enter or leave the market.
- There are many buyers and sellers of the product.
- There are no government restrictions.
- No one buyer or seller can control the price of the product.

In most cases, competition in the market is less than perfect. Few products are bought and sold in markets that resemble perfect competition. Exceptions include some agricultural products, such as wheat.

19. What is perfect competition?

_____

_____

20. Why do you think perfect competition is difficult to achieve?

_____

_____

_____

✔*Check Your Understanding*

Suppose Schwinn sells Classic Cruisers to you and to two other dealers for $150 each. At Classic Bicycles, you set your selling price at $250. You see in a newspaper ad that Bixby's Bikes is selling Classic Cruisers for $450.

21. For each Classic Cruiser sold, who will make more profit—Bixby's Bikes or Classic Bicycles, considering that their costs are the same?

_____

22. Predict who will sell more Classic Cruisers—Classic Bicycles or Bixby's Bikes. Explain your prediction.

_____

_____

23. Charlene's Cycles offers Classic Cruisers for $160 each. Predict how Charlene's sales will compare to those of Classic Bicycles. Explain your prediction.

_____

_____

24. Predict how the market price for Classic Cruisers will change over the long run. What do you think the final price for a Classic Cruiser at Classic Bicycles will be? Explain your prediction.

_____

_____

Monopolies

Suppose your bicycle shop is the only one that sells restored Black Phantoms. You then have a monopoly on restored Black Phantoms. A **monopoly** exists when a single seller sells a product. Because there is no competition, a monopolist may charge the highest price consumers are willing to pay. A monopoly is the opposite of perfect competition. In perfect competition, sellers sell products at the same price.

In a monopoly:

- The market has only one producer.
- That producer controls the price for the product.
- There are no substitutes for the product.
- Other producers are not free to enter the market because there are barriers, often set by a government, to other companies from entering the market.

Setting prices in a monopoly is tricky, however. You still need to worry about demand. At high prices, you may think that you can make a big profit on each Black Phantom that you sell. However, you may charge so much that people won't be willing (or able) to buy Black Phantoms.

25. What is a monopoly?

_____

_____

26. What does the single seller in a monopoly have to consider when setting prices?

_____

_____

_____

Legal Monopolies

The United States government has outlawed most monopolies. It does allow these three types of monopolies to exist: geographical monopolies, natural monopolies, and technological monopolies.

Geographical Monopoly Imagine being the only store that sells bicycle tires for miles around. Tire prices are normally set by competition. Because you are the only tire dealer around, however, you have a monopoly on prices.

Natural Monopoly Natural monopolies exist if it is inefficient to have more than one seller. Therefore, the law allows some corporations, such as electrical power companies, to be monopolies. Power companies need billions of dollars in capital to get started. With so much at stake, it is difficult for others to enter the industry and compete with large, existing companies. For these reasons, the law allows power companies to be monopolies. To control prices, state governments make rules about how much monopolies can charge.

Technological Monopoly Suppose you invented a new bicycle tire that won't go flat. You can protect your invention with a patent. A **patent** is a license issued by the federal government that gives you and only you the rights over your invention. Using your patent, you are free to set prices at whatever level the market will bear.

27. What are three types of legal monopolies?

_____

_____

_____

28. How do patents encourage people to invent new things?

_____

_____

Imperfect Competition

We have looked at perfect competition and monopolies, but many industries fall somewhere between the two. These industries exist in a state of imperfect competition. Here are two types of imperfect competition.

Monopolistic Competition All aspirin may be identical. Some brands of aspirin, however, make claims that they are different from the others. Over time, companies convince customers that their brand of aspirin is unique and special. Customers could buy substitute products, but they don't, so brands gain some monopoly power on the strength of their own name and reputation. For loyal consumers, there is no substitute for the product, even though many other products may work just as well.

Oligopoly When a market is dominated by a few competitors, it is an **oligopoly**. The soft drink market is an example of an oligopoly. Two or three producers control a huge percentage of soft drink sales.

In some cases, oligopolies can be very competitive. Producers set prices independently. This competition keeps prices down. Sometimes, producers follow prices set by the industry leader. In some cases, competitors may try to fix prices. They try to make secret agreements to keep prices high. Price fixing is illegal in the United States.

29. What is an oligopoly?

_____

_____

30. In what ways are prices set in an oligopoly?

_____

_____

_____

31. Describe monopolistic competition. Use a different example from the one used in the text.

_____

_____

_____

Think About It!

Circle graphs provide one way of looking at data. The graphs below compare sole proprietorships, partnerships, and corporations in terms of sales and profits. Study the graphs and answer the following questions.

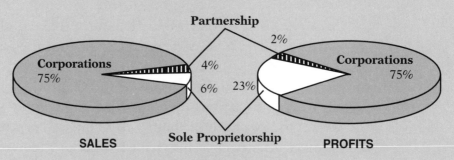

32. Which type of business structure had the most sales?

_____

33. Which type of business structure had the fewest sales?

_____

34. For sole proprietorships, how do profits compare with sales?

_____

35. For corporations, how do profits compare with sales?

_____

_____

Reading a Line Graph

A line graph helps you keep track of how a set of data changes over time. The line graph below charts how Schwinn's share of the bicycle market changed from 1983 to 1992.

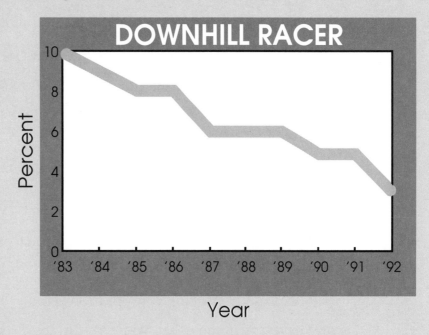

To read the line graph, line up a point with both the horizontal and vertical axes. For example, the upper left point lines up with 10 percent on the vertical scale and the year 1983 on the horizontal scale. This means that Schwinn had 10 percent of the bicycle market in 1983.

Use the graph to answer the following questions.

1. What was Schwinn's market share in 1986?

_____

2. In what year did Schwinn have 6 percent of the market?

_____

3. What was the low point in market share for Schwinn? When did this low point occur?

_____

4. What general trend do you see in Schwinn's share of the market during this time period? Is it going up or down?

_____

5. Why do you think Schwinn declared bankruptcy in 1992?

_____

Vocabulary

Complete each sentence with a term from the list below.

| CEO | partnership | financial capital | sole proprietor |
| interest | monopoly | charter | perfect competition |

1. One type of _____ is a sum of money used to start a business.

2. The opposite of a monopoly is _____.

3. A corporation must get a _____ in order to do business as a corporation.

4. A person who owns his or her own business is called a _____.

5. The person who runs a corporation is the _____.

6. The extra money that you pay for the privilege of using others' money is _____.

7. People join together to form a business _____.

8. A _____ exists when a single seller sells a product.

Main Idea

Answer the following questions.

9. What are the three main types of business structures?

_____

_____

_____

_____

10. What are the characteristics of perfect competition?

_____

_____

_____

_____

11. Why do you think most monopolies are illegal in the United States?

_____

_____

Understanding Economics

12. Suppose you owned 50 percent of a corporation that needed money. To raise money, you could either issue corporate bonds or issue some stock. Which option would you prefer? Explain your answer.

_____

_____

_____

13. Congress is considering tightening the laws so that companies would be less monopolistic. How do you think consumer groups would feel about this change? Explain.

_____

_____

_____

14. Suppose your corporation offered new shares of stock for sale at $50 per share, and few people bought the stock. What could you do to get people to buy your corporation's stocks?

_____

_____

_____

Project

Organize a class corporation. First, apply to your teacher for a charter. In your charter application, give the name of your corporation, explain its purpose and goals, and describe the products that it will make. After you receive your charter, hold elections among the members of the class (stockholders) for a three-person board of directors. Let the board of directors appoint a CEO, vice-presidents, and department heads. Then make an organizational chart for your corporation.

In 1988, Mitch Curren was no ice-cream expert. She knew very little about the ice-cream business. She knew even less about Ben & Jerry's ice-cream company. To tell the truth, Curren didn't even like ice cream very much. So how did Curren get to be Ben & Jerry's "Info Queen"? How did she become the world's number-one authority on Vermont's most famous ice-cream company?

"Actually, I already had a job when I applied at Ben & Jerry's," Curren recalled. At the time, she was a writing instructor at Vermont State College. It was a good job, but it didn't pay very well. Curren decided that she needed another job to make ends meet. So she scanned the help-wanted pages of a local newspaper. It was there that she came across the ad for a tour-guide job at Ben & Jerry's ice-cream factory. It said:

GAIN 62 POUNDS IN 3 WEEKS!

Curren thought this statement was hilarious. "That ad sounded so interesting and fun that I knew I just had to apply," she said. So Curren prepared her resume. In it, she listed her qualifications. She had a master's degree in English from the State University of New York, Binghamton. She had worked as a part-time English teacher and also as a judo instructor.

The Tour

None of Curren's job qualifications were especially impressive to the people at Ben & Jerry's. They didn't care much about grades or degrees. They were interested in Curren's speaking and communication skills. Almost immediately, they spotted her potential as a tour guide.

The only problem was that Curren couldn't see herself as a tour guide. "I was terrified at the very idea of doing things I had never done before," Curren said. So she decided not to apply for the tour guide job. Instead, she applied for a job in the gift shop at Ben &

> *What does Ben & Jerry's "Info Queen" do?*

COME TO WORK FOR VERMONT'S FINEST.

Ben and Jerry's is looking for highly motivated, quality conscious team players to fill the following positions at our Waterbury facility.

There is a growing benefit package for permanent, fulltime employees that includes 3 free pints of ice cream per day, profit sharing, 100% employer-paid health, dental, long-term disability and life insurance, two weeks paid vacation per calendar year, paid holidays, employee stock purchase plan, health club and credit union memberships, company outings, and more! The company reviews hourly employees every six months. Raises are based on performance.

GAIN 62 POUNDS IN 3 WEEKS!
...or perhaps you can resist the temptation to eat your 3 free pints a day if we hire you to work in our Waterbury store. We have positions available giving tours, and in our scoop and retail shops. Starting wages are between $5.00/hr.–$6.50/hr. Part-time, full-time, permanent, and seasonal positions available. Please drop in and see us for an interview.

★★★★★★★★★★★★★★★★★★★★
DO YOU REMEMBER LUCY AND ETHEL ON THE CANDY LINE?
Well, we're not exactly like that. But, now that we have your attention, we invite you to apply for full-time work on our production and freezer/warehouse teams. Day and night shifts available. $6.50/hr. to start. Call us or come in for an interview anytime.

Ben & Jerry's ad writers use unusual ads to attract job applicants.

Jerry's. When the job interviewer sent her to the Tour Department, Curren was sure that they were making a mistake.

"No mistake," they told her. So Curren took a tour with one of the experienced guides. The tour was fun and interesting. Curren asked a lot of questions. She smiled. She was enthusiastic. Little did she know that these were just the qualities that the Ben & Jerry's officials were looking for in a tour guide.

Even though Curren kept insisting that she wouldn't be a good tour guide, the people at Ben & Jerry's weren't convinced. In the end, they offered her the tour-guide job for $6.50 an hour. "I can now look back and honestly say that it was one of the best jobs I never wanted," Curren laughed.

Ben & Jerry's ice-cream lovers can stop in for a quick cone at over 100 franchise "scoop shops" located in 20 states around the country.

Tour-Guide Days

After being hired, Curren went to a sort of ice-cream "boot camp" for new tour guides. During this time, Curren learned a lot about Ben & Jerry's. For three days, she worked as an ice-cream maker—scooping, dipping, and dunking. Afterward, Curren felt quite sore, but she had learned some valuable facts about making ice cream. She had also gained a deep respect for the people who make the ice cream.

This training helped Curren in her new job. She quickly became one of Ben & Jerry's best tour guides. After two years, Curren was a pro. She was ready to go on to bigger jobs. Curren then transferred to Ben & Jerry's Marketing Department. As an assistant to the marketing director, Curren learned even more about Ben & Jerry's ice cream, including how it was advertised, distributed, and made its way into new markets.

Then one day, the marketing director left the company. Suddenly, Curren had nothing to do. She was the assistant to the marketing director, but the company no longer had one. It was not planning on filling the position in the near future, either.

New Challenges

The people at Ben & Jerry's wanted to keep Curren. So they moved her to the Public Relations Department. There, Curren became deeply involved in promoting Ben & Jerry's unusual business ideas. How unusual are Ben & Jerry's ideas? Jerry Greenfield, the "Jerry" of Ben & Jerry's said: "We think making a better world increases profits."

Curren soon learned how Ben & Jerry's puts its money where its mouth is. It works to make a "better world" in many ways, including:

- giving 7.5 percent of company profits to charity

- thinking of new ways to prevent industrial pollution

- helping environmental groups

- recycling

- ordering ingredients, such as brownies, from companies that employ homeless and disadvantaged people

- using milk from small family-run dairy farms

- treating employees with dignity and respect

Creating Her Own Job

At the time that Curren started working in the Public Relations Department, Ben & Jerry's was beginning to create a real stir in the business community. Suddenly, businesses all over the country wanted to know about Ben & Jerry's socially responsible business practices. Students called, wanting to know how they could help. Teachers and professors called, wanting to know how they could use Ben & Jerry's ideas in the classroom. Individual citizens called, wanting to know how they could use Ben & Jerry's ideas to bring change on a broader scale.

Boyhood friends, Ben Cohen, left, and Jerry Greenfield, started their ice-cream business in a renovated gas station in 1978.

At first, various people in the Public Relations Department handled these calls. But over time, they realized that there was one person in the office who handled the calls best—Mitch Curren. Curren became known as Ben & Jerry's "Info Queen." Whenever people had questions about Ben & Jerry's, they were referred to Curren.

Curren still isn't sure if she invented her job or if the job invented her. What she does know is that Ben & Jerry's gets almost 5,000 calls and letters a year asking for information. The callers range from second-graders to professional researchers. Curren handles almost every one of these calls and letters herself. She tirelessly gives out information about everything from Cherry Garcia ice-cream ingredients to Ben's famous ability to invent new ice-cream flavors.

Ben & Jerry's "Info Queen," Mitch Curren, dispenses facts and figures from her office in Waterbury, Vermont.

Over time, Curren has expanded her job by thinking of new ways to communicate Ben & Jerry's message. She has created an on-line computer network for interacting with Ben & Jerry's customers. She gives speeches, throws parties, writes pamphlets, and thinks up goofy ideas to promote Ben & Jerry's "caring capitalism."

Curren is quite clear about the future: "Whether our velvet hammer and whoopie cushion approach to socially responsible business education would work elsewhere, or even whether it will continue to work here, is anyone's guess," she said. "If there's something other companies can realize from our example, it is that a company's possibilities for being profitable and socially responsible are as unlimited as its willingness to explore them."

In Chapter 1, you learned that goods are products that people use. Ben & Jerry's makes a product that people use. You also learned that services are activities that people perform for other people. Curren performs a service by answering the public's questions about Ben & Jerry's.

Skilled and Unskilled Workers

Mitch Curren works. This fact makes her part of the labor force of the United States. The **labor force** is the total number of people over the age of 16 who are employed or are actively seeking work. Farm workers made up the majority of the U.S. labor force in the early 1800s. However, today the kind of work people do has changed. Most jobs are in cities, not on farms. Non-farm workers fall into two categories: those who produce goods and those who perform services.

1. What is the labor force?

_____

_____

_____

2. How has the U.S. labor force changed since the early 1800s?

_____

_____

_____

White-Collar and Blue-Collar Workers

Jobs in the labor force can be separated into two categories: white-collar jobs and blue-collar jobs. **Blue-collar workers** generally perform "physical work"—often in factories—and are not required to be college graduates. Mechanics, factory workers, and laborers are blue-collar workers. So are bus drivers, repair people, and cleaners. **White-collar workers** generally perform "mental work"—usually in offices. They are usually college graduates. They include doctors, lawyers, teachers, and business executives. These people are also called professionals. **Professionals** are people who generally have graduate degrees and are certified to work in their field as a result of passing special tests.

Some blue-collar workers produce goods; others provide services. Think about the employees at Ben & Jerry's. The blue-collar worker making the ice cream is producing goods. The blue-collar worker repairing the ice-cream machines is performing a service.

White-collar workers usually provide services. They often supervise other workers. A white-collar salesperson provides the service of selling Ben & Jerry's ice cream to grocery store chains.

3. Does Curren have a white-collar job or a blue-collar job? Explain.

_____

_____

4. Do the workers who manufacture ice cream at the Ben & Jerry's plant have white-collar jobs or blue-collar jobs? Explain.

_____

_____

Comparing White-Collar and Blue-Collar Workers

The chart below compares white-collar workers to blue-collar workers. In general, white-collar workers have more training or education. They also have broader responsibilities and make a higher wage than blue-collar workers. There are many exceptions, however, to these generalizations, as shown on the chart below. Use the chart to answer the questions on the next page.

	Require a lot of training?	EXAMPLE	EXCEPTION
WHITE-COLLAR WORKERS	YES	Architects need several years of training.	Office workers need limited training.
BLUE-COLLAR WORKERS	NO	Factory workers need limited training.	Master carpenters are highly trained.
	Have a lot of responsibility?	EXAMPLE	EXCEPTION
WHITE-COLLAR WORKERS	YES	Doctors are responsible for people's lives.	Computer operators are responsible for their work only.
BLUE-COLLAR WORKERS	NO	Factory workers are responsible for their work only.	Train engineers are responsible for people's lives.
	Get a lot of pay?	EXAMPLE	EXCEPTION
WHITE-COLLAR WORKERS	YES	Lawyers can make very high salaries.	Some sales clerks receive the minimum wage.
BLUE-COLLAR WORKERS	NO	Some laborers earn the minimum wage.	Plumbers can earn high wages.

5. What kind of blue-collar worker is usually highly trained?

_____

_____

_____

6. Do white-collar workers or blue-collar workers usually have broader responsibilities?

_____

_____

A chart can help you compare pieces of information quickly. Look at the chart. Read the title and labels to see what information is given.

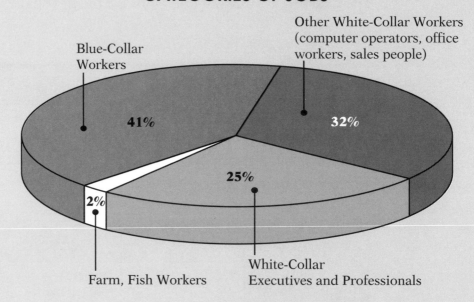

CATEGORIES OF JOBS

Blue-Collar Workers — 41%

Other White-Collar Workers (computer operators, office workers, sales people) — 32%

White-Collar Executives and Professionals — 25%

Farm, Fish Workers — 2%

7. Which job category has the highest percentage of workers?

_____

8. Which job category has the lowest percentage of workers?

_____

9. White-collar professionals and other white-collar workers together make up about what percentage of the labor force?

_____

Skill Levels

Another way to look at the labor force is by skill level. A **skill level** indicates the amount of training and schooling that a worker has received.

Unskilled Workers These workers perform jobs that require little training and education. Laborers and cleaners are examples of unskilled workers. Unskilled workers are usually easy for employers to replace. For this reason, they generally receive low pay.

Semi-skilled Workers Jobs that require some education and training are often done by semi-skilled workers. Office workers and machine operators are examples of semi-skilled workers. Semi-skilled workers are more difficult to replace than unskilled workers. They generally receive low to medium pay.

Skilled Workers Highly skilled workers, including computer technicians and electricians, have jobs that require special training and education. Skilled workers are often difficult to replace. They generally receive medium to high pay. Some other skilled workers are carpenters, x-ray technicians, and crane operators.

Professionals These highly trained people have college degrees and often have further training beyond that. Dentists, lawyers, and business executives are examples of professionals. Professionals are difficult to replace. Professionals usually receive very high pay.

10. Which type of worker generally receives the highest pay? Why?

_____

_____

_____

11. Which type of worker generally has the least training and education?

_____

_____

_____

12. Which types of workers are generally the most difficult to replace?

_____

_____

_____

✔ Check Your Understanding

Review the four types of workers. Then complete the chart below.

WORKER CATEGORIES

TYPE OF WORKER	EDUCATION AND TRAINING	EASY TO REPLACE?	PAY RANGE
UNSKILLED	Low	Yes	13. _____
SEMI-SKILLED	Low to Medium	14. _____	15. _____
SKILLED	16. _____	No	17. _____
PROFESSIONAL	Very High	18. _____	19. _____

The Trouble with Categories

Categories, such as skilled and unskilled, can be useful for learning about the work force. But they can also be misleading. Take the case of Mitch Curren. Before she began working at Ben & Jerry's, Curren had a professional job. She had a master's degree in English. Yet, the pay that Curren received as a part-time English instructor "was not enough to live on," she said. Even though she was a professional, Curren did not have a high-paying job. Then Curren became the "Info Queen." Being "Info Queen" does not require a master's degree, but the job pays Curren more money than she made teaching.

20. Why are skill level categories misleading?

_____

_____

Supply and Demand in the Labor Market

In Chapter 3, you learned about supply and demand for goods and services. Supply and demand also play key roles in the labor market. Think back to the definitions of supply and demand. Remember that supply is how much producers are willing and able to sell at different prices in a given period of time. Demand is how much consumers are willing and able to buy at different prices in a given period of time. In the labor market, the product is labor itself; therefore:

- Supply is the willingness of workers to sell their labor at given prices.

- Demand is the willingness of businesses to buy that labor at given prices.

In the case of Mitch Curren, Ben & Jerry's was the buyer of Curren's labor. Curren was the seller of her labor. Ben & Jerry's had a demand for workers. Its want ad offered to buy Curren's labor for a certain price. In taking the job, Curren sold her labor to Ben & Jerry's for $6.50 an hour.

21. In the labor market, who is the buyer? the seller?

_____

_____

How Demand Affects Pay

To understand how demand affects pay, imagine that you have $20 to spend on ice-cream cake. You can buy one very expensive $20 ice-cream cake, two $10 cakes, or four $5 cakes. You base your decision on how many cakes you need and the quality of the cakes.

Suppose you have another $20 to spend. This time you are not buying cake. You are buying an hour's worth of labor. You might be willing to hire four workers at $5 per hour, two workers at $10 per hour, or one worker at $20 per hour. As the price of labor goes up, your willingness to pay the price for it will change. In other words, the higher the price of labor, the less of that labor will be hired. This is the law of demand that you learned about in Chapter 3. Of course, sometimes there are exceptions. There are times when you need high-priced labor because the job requires it.

22. How does the amount that people are paid affect their chances of being hired?

_____

_____

23. Buyers of goods want to pay as little as they can for them. How are buyers of labor similar to buyers of goods?

_____

_____

How Supply Affects Pay

Now suppose you are selling ice-cream cake instead of buying it. The more that people are willing to pay for ice-cream cake, the more willing you are to supply it. The same situation holds for labor. When employers are willing to pay more for workers, more workers are willing to work.

At $5 per hour, only a few workers might apply for a job. At $10 per hour, the job is more attractive. At $20 per hour, almost everyone wants the job. The higher the pay offered, the more workers a job attracts. This is the law of supply. In this case, it says that the higher wages go, the more the supply of labor will increase.

24. How does the price of labor, or pay, affect labor supply?

_____

_____

Other Factors that Affect Pay

Both supply and demand affect the price of labor. As buyers, employers try to pay as little as they can for labor. As sellers, workers try to get as much as they can for their work. In the end, a balance is reached between buyers and sellers, and a labor price, or pay level, is set.

Three other factors related to supply and demand—skill, job type, and job location—also very much affect how much workers are paid.

Skill In many cases, employers need more than just a worker. They need someone with a special talent. For example, Curren has a special talent. She is very good at public relations. Curren has special skills that can't easily be replaced. That is why she earns more now than when she was a tour guide. To get someone with special skills, an employer must pay more.

Job Type The wages offered in Ben & Jerry's want ad didn't seem very high to Mitch Curren. But the job sounded like fun. So Curren was willing to make less money for a job that she would enjoy. In a similar way, job type can affect wages. Fighting forest fires is dangerous and difficult work. For this reason, fire fighters get higher wages.

Job Location Suppose Ben & Jerry's wanted to transfer Mitch Curren to its new plant in Alaska. Company leaders might need to offer Curren higher pay. Why? Because Curren likes it in Vermont, she might not want to move to Alaska. Also, the cost of living in

Alaska is high. To persuade her to go there, Ben & Jerry's would have to pay her more money. In addition, few people live in Alaska. To attract other workers, Ben & Jerry's might need to offer much higher than usual pay.

25. How does skill affect pay?

_____

_____

26. How does job location affect pay?

_____

_____

Demanding Higher Pay

Suppose Mitch Curren wants a raise. She could ask her supervisor for higher pay. The supervisor might give Curren a raise, or the supervisor might not. Curren would need to make a decision: Should she keep on working for her current pay, try to renegotiate higher pay, or look for a new job?

In Curren's case, renegotiating might work. Curren is a unique person with special skills. Ben & Jerry's might not be able to replace her easily. But for many workers, trying to renegotiate might not work. Employers often think that certain workers are easy to replace.

27. Why is Curren in a good position to renegotiate for higher pay?

_____

_____

Labor Unions

Individual workers sometimes have little power. They can try to negotiate with their employers for higher pay, but they may be unsuccessful. In groups, workers may gain power. Suppose a group of workers got together and demanded higher pay. Now, the employer wouldn't be able to ignore them so easily because it may be too difficult to replace them all.

Groups of workers sometimes band together to form **labor unions**. In the late 1800s, many labor unions arose in the United States. Union workers demanded higher pay and shorter hours. If their demands weren't met, they stopped working. They went on strike.

Most of the early strikes were unsuccessful. The employers fired the strikers. Then they hired new workers to take their places. The fired workers tried to stop the new ones from taking their jobs. Violence broke out. The government stepped in to stop the violence. Until the early 1900s, the government usually sided with the employers. Workers were given one choice: Go back to work or lose your job.

28. What is a labor union?

_____

_____

_____

Unions Gain Power

Slowly, laws and attitudes about unions changed. The government recognized workers' rights to form labor unions and to go on strike. The unions used this power to gain higher wages and better working conditions. These changes were sorely needed. Before the rise of labor unions, factories were dangerous. Many people worked 14 hours a day for very low wages.

Unions went on strike to change the labor market. For the most part, they were successful. Wages went up. Working conditions in factories improved. The standard workday decreased to eight hours. Children went to school instead of to work. The unions became almost as powerful as the companies that they bargained with.

Today there are laws that protect workers. For example, it is now illegal for employers to practice **discrimination**. To discriminate means to judge someone based on a characteristic, such as age, ethnicity, gender, or religion. It is illegal for employers to reject a job applicant on the basis of age, ethnicity, gender, or religion.

29. What were working conditions like before labor unions existed?

_____

_____

_____

30. How did unions change the lives of workers?

_____

_____

_____

_____

Think About It!

In Chapter 4, you learned that a minimum wage law was enacted in 1938. Union power helped pass that law. Minimum wage, the lowest amount that an employer can pay a worker, was 75 cents an hour in 1950. By 1991, the minimum wage had risen to $4.25 an hour. Many people believe that today's minimum wage should be increased to reflect increases in the cost of living. The **cost of living** is the price of basic needs, such as housing, food, and clothing.

31. What might employers think about a minimum wage increase?

_____

_____

_____

32. Some people believe that a minimum wage increase would cause many people to lose their jobs. Why might this occur?

_____

_____

Getting a Paycheck

Suppose you just landed a $10-an-hour job at Ben & Jerry's. In your first week, you worked 40 hours. According to your calculations, you should receive:

$$\$10 \text{ per hour} \times 40 \text{ hours} = \$400$$

But when you open the pay envelope, you are shocked. The check is made out for $252.09! What happened to the other $147.91? To understand, you need to learn more about deductions. Deductions, as you read in Chapter 4, are taxes and expenses that are subtracted from your gross pay. Your **gross pay** is the total amount of money that you earn before the deductions are subtracted.

Your **net pay** is the amount left after the deductions have been subtracted from your gross pay. Net pay is your "take-home pay"— the actual amount of money that you receive.

33. What are deductions?

_____

_____

Understanding Deductions

As you learned in Chapter 4, people pay income tax to support the government. Income tax, a deduction, is based on a person's salary. The more money a person makes, the more income tax a person pays. There are many types of deductions as shown below:

Federal Income Tax This is a tax that workers pay to support the federal government. Federal income tax pays for such services as national defense and the upkeep of national parks.

State Income Tax This is a tax that workers pay to support many state governments. For example, the upkeep of state highways is paid for by state taxes. Not all states have a state income tax.

FICA The Federal Insurance Contributions Act, or FICA, is called the Social Security tax. Social Security is mainly a retirement program. When U.S. workers retire, many receive a Social Security pension from the government. A **pension** is money paid regularly to a person upon his or her retirement. Social Security pensions are paid for by Social Security taxes. Also, if a worker gets sick or injured and cannot work, the government will pay him or her Social Security benefits to help with rent, food, and other expenses.

Medicare Tax Medicare is an insurance fund that helps pay medical bills for people over the age of 65.

Medical Insurance Medical insurance helps people under 65 years of age afford the high cost of medical care. In some cases, employers pay part or all of the cost of a worker's medical insurance. The amount taken out as a deduction is the part of the medical insurance that the worker pays.

401K The 401K is a special kind of retirement savings program. Unlike Social Security, workers can choose to pay money into a 401K plan. They can also choose how their money is invested. If they choose wisely, the money will earn interest and increase in value. Most employers match at least part of a worker's 401K contributions.

34. What is income tax?

_____

_____

35. Name two deductions that are for retirement programs. How are these two programs different from one another?

_____

_____

Reading a Pay Stub

Each paycheck that a worker receives is attached to a pay stub. A **pay stub** is a record of a worker's gross pay and deductions for a particular pay period. Take a look at the following pay stub.

Earnings	Rate x Hours	Gross Pay
	$10 x 40	$400
Mandatory Deductions	**Type**	**Amount**
	Federal Income Tax	$40.96
	FICA (Social Security Tax)	$24.03
	Medicare Tax	$5.62
	State Income Tax	$10.24
Voluntary Deductions	**Type**	**Amount**
	Medical Insurance	$19.00
	401K	$48.06
	Total Deductions	**$147.91**
	Net Pay	**$252.09**

The first section lists your earnings. It gives your hours, rate of pay, and gross pay. The second section lists deductions. The first four deductions are mandatory, which means that the government says that you must pay them. The deductions in the second group are voluntary. You have chosen to have them deducted from your pay. The final two lines list the total amount of all your deductions and your net, or actual, pay.

Use the pay stub to answer the following questions.

1. What is the gross pay?

_____

2. What is the largest mandatory deduction?

_____

3. What is the largest voluntary deduction?

_____

4. How much less is being withheld for state income tax than for federal income tax?

_____

5. What is the total amount paid in taxes?

_____

Vocabulary

Complete each sentence with a term from the list below.

discriminate	labor union	professionals
blue-collar workers	gross pay	net pay
pension	labor force	

1. _____ is also called take-home pay.

2. _____ perform jobs that require little training and education.

3. Highly skilled workers are also called _____.

4. The total amount of money that you earn before deductions are taken out is your _____.

5. To _____ means to judge someone based on a characteristic, such as age, gender, or ethnicity.

6. A _____ is money paid regularly to a person upon his or her retirement.

7. The total number of people over age 16 who are employed or are actively seeking work is the _____.

8. A group formed by workers who band together is called a _____.

Main Idea

Answer the following questions.

9. What job categories are there in the labor force?

_____

_____

10. What factors affect pay?

_____

_____

11. What deductions appear on every pay stub?

_____

_____

_____

_____

Understanding Economics

12. A major company closes its factory in Vermont. Explain how this closing will affect supply and demand in the Vermont labor market.

_____

_____

_____

_____

13. Suppose all of Ben & Jerry's employees go on strike and demand higher pay. Ben & Jerry's officials can: 1) give in to the workers' demands; 2) try to negotiate to reach a compromise; or 3) fire the strikers and replace them with other workers. Explain the advantages and the disadvantages of each option. Then tell which option you would choose and why.

_____

_____

_____

_____

Project

With a group of classmates, look through the want ads in your local newspaper. While you are looking at the jobs offered, think about the skills that each requires. Compare the pay offered for the various jobs. Discuss whether the pay seems fair. Together, make a list of jobs for which you would like to apply.

When Sarah Peters was growing up in Arlington, Texas, money wasn't a problem. Her parents earned enough to pay their bills and raise their children. The family certainly wasn't wealthy, but her parents never stayed up nights worrying about money. So Sarah is still surprised at her own money troubles. She ended up thousands of dollars in debt. In fact, she owed so much money that she had little hope of ever getting out of debt. It all started in college with credit cards.

How will Sarah dig her way out of debt?

After high school, Sarah stayed in her hometown and attended the University of Texas at Arlington. That way she could continue to live at home with her parents. They supported her; they paid her living expenses, her college tuition, and car payments. Sarah had a part-time job at a photo shop during college. The money from that job paid for clothes and for hanging out with friends. For a year and a half, all was well.

The Seeds of a Problem

During Sarah's sophomore year, she received an American Express credit card in the mail. Now she didn't have to worry about carrying cash when she went out. She could buy a skirt and pay for it with a little plastic card. She could rent videos and charge them. Not only was it convenient, but it also made her feel like an adult.

Sarah's American Express bill came once every month. It had to be paid in full within the month. This monthly payment arrangement wasn't a problem for Sarah. She was careful with her purchases. She kept track of how much she charged. Every month, she wrote out a check to American Express.

The next year, MasterCard sent Sarah a credit card, too. Whenever she shopped for clothes, she had a choice of credit cards. But now she had

The only thing Sarah Peters loves better than shopping is the ease and convenience of paying for her purchases with a credit card.

to keep track of how much she charged on each card. She had to send out two checks every month. Her MasterCard, though, didn't require her to pay off the full balance every month. If she couldn't pay the whole amount one month, she could just pay part of it. The rest of the amount that she owed would be put on the next month's bill. Sarah could now buy what she wanted even if she didn't have enough money for it. "What a great setup!" Sarah thought.

What Sarah wasn't thinking about was that the credit card company would charge her interest on the unpaid balance. Interest is money paid for the use of someone else's money. When Sarah bought items on credit, she was actually borrowing money from the credit card company to pay for them. Because interest rates on credit cards can be high, the unpaid balance on Sarah's credit card account went up very quickly.

Debt Takes Root

Soon, Sarah received other credit cards: an Optima card, a Discover card, and another MasterCard. Her wallet bulged with them. On some of the cards, she kept small balances. These balances stayed on her bills month after month. Even though the amounts that Sarah owed were small, the interest charges weren't. Every month, most of her pay from the photo shop went to the credit card companies.

Then Sarah graduated from college. At this point, her money troubles really began. For the first time in her life, Sarah was on her own. She moved to Austin, Texas, and found a job and an apartment. Suddenly, she was flooded with bills. She had to pay her own rent, car payments, and car insurance. She also had to buy food, clothing, and other necessities. Her parents were no longer paying her expenses. She could definately feel the strain of living on her own.

There are bank cards, gasoline cards, and department store cards. The company or bank name, the cardholder's name, the account number, and the expiration date are printed on the front.

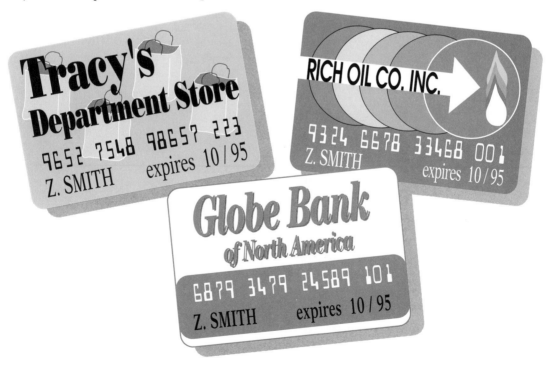

A fun-filled trip to Europe, including a visit to France's Eiffel Tower, put Sarah even deeper into credit card debt.

would go: San Francisco, New York City, Mexico, Guatemala, Paris, Jamaica. These were all places that she wanted to see. Within a few years, Sarah had traveled to them all. How could she afford to pay for trips and new clothes? The answer is credit cards, of course.

Before very long, Sarah owed many thousands of dollars to the credit card companies. Every month, she could pay only the minimum amount that each credit card account required. Still, she kept traveling every year and charging the trips. Her credit card bills kept growing. Sarah had never learned how to manage her money. Soon, though, she would be forced to learn that lesson.

Sarah's bills grew so large that she couldn't afford even the minimum required payments. She started to miss payments. Her creditors—all the people to whom she owed money—started to call her. They wanted their money, but Sarah didn't have it. She was working full-time at a good job, but she didn't have enough money to make payments on all of her debts.

Living the Good Life

Sarah found that the money she made at her job was just enough to cover rent, car payments, insurance, and household expenses. There was little left over for clothing or for entertainment. But Sarah loved to shop. She liked to have nice clothes for work. So she bought them. She also loved to travel. Her job gave her two weeks vacation a year. She spent the other 50 weeks planning where she

Slowly Digging Out

Sarah was in over her head. She didn't even know how much money she owed. She did know, though, that she needed

Sarah and her credit counselor discuss a payment plan and a budget in order to reduce Sarah's $19,000 credit card debt.

help. So, in late 1992, she went to a company called Consumer Credit Counseling. Together, she and a credit counselor went through her financial records. They looked at all of Sarah's household and credit card bills. They also looked at her income tax returns and her pay stubs.

The credit counselor discovered that Sarah owed a total of $19,000— $6,000 of which was what she still owed on her car. They calculated that she could afford to pay about $400 each month for debt payments. They arranged for Sarah to send the $400 directly to Consumer Credit Counseling each month. After subtracting its own fee, the company would then transmit portions of the remainder of the $400 to Sarah's creditors.

Sarah kept to this payment schedule for some time. In 1993, she moved to Boston. She didn't need to drive in the city and sold her car for $8,000. She paid off her car loan and used the rest to pay off more of her debts. Now she was about $6,000 in debt. She continued sending $400 every month to Consumer Credit Counseling to pay off the remainder of her debt.

Two long years later, Sarah was finally out of debt. Today Sarah is very careful about the purchases that she makes, especially credit card purchases. She has learned a very difficult lesson.

Exchange, Money, and Interdependence

Imagine a world without money. There would be no debts, no bills to worry about, and no financial problems. It would be great, wouldn't it? Or would it? Without money, how would you get the goods and services that you need? How would you eat? Where would you live? Sure, you could try making it on your own. For example, you could build your own house. But where would you get the materials? Sooner or later, you would need something that someone else made or owned.

In all economic systems, people trade, or **exchange**, goods and services. Sometimes they trade for other goods and services, and sometimes they trade for money. Early societies didn't use money as we know it today. Instead, they used a barter system. **Barter**—the direct trading of one good for another—is the simplest form of exchange. For example, someone who raises chickens might trade with someone who grows rice. This way, both can have chicken and rice for dinner.

What happens, though, if the rice grower no longer wants chickens? Then the chicken farmer must find someone else with whom to trade and may end up with goods that he or she doesn't want. For example, a nearby sheep rancher wants to trade wool for chickens, but the chicken farmer needs grain, not wool. This is just one of the difficulties in a barter system. Barter is usually not an efficient means of exchange.

1. What is a barter system?

_____

_____

What if the chicken farmer and the rice grower both exchanged their goods for some third type of good? What if this good, in turn, could easily be traded for any other good or service? This good would then be a form of money. **Money** is something that can be used to buy all types of goods and services. Money functions as:

- a medium of exchange
- a unit of value
- a store of value

A Medium of Exchange In a barter system, you usually end up with some goods that you don't need. In a money system, though, you first trade goods and services for money. Then you trade the money for goods and services that you want.

A Unit of Value In a barter system, you must decide again and again how much your goods are worth. How many pounds of rice is a large chicken worth? How many shoes is that same chicken worth? In a money system, money is the standard unit of value for all goods and services. A chicken is worth a certain number of dollars and cents. Once you sell the chicken, you can exchange those dollars for so many pounds of rice or so many shoes.

A Store of Value In a barter system, you must always be aware of how long the goods that you are trading for will last. For example, if you trade your goods for food, the food may spoil before you can eat it. If you trade for money, though, you can keep the money until you need other goods. You can buy as much food as you need today, and then buy more tomorrow. The money stores the value of the goods that you sold. You can hold on to this stored value as long as you wish.

2. What are the three functions of money?

_____

_____

_____

3. What are the disadvantages of using the barter system?

_____

_____

_____

4. How does money function as a store of value?

_____

_____

Characteristics of Money

Throughout history, different societies have used different items for money. Feathers, salt, fish hooks, pigs, and shells have all been used as money. In the 1600s, some Native Americans fashioned small shells into beads called wampum. They traded these beads to European colonists, who in turn used the wampum as a form of money. To be used as money, an item should be:

- durable
- portable
- divisible
- stable

Durable Any item used for money should be able to stand up to hard use. Fish hooks and wampum were very durable. Feathers probably didn't last as long. Paper bills and metal coins are fairly sturdy and can last a long time.

Portable To serve as money, items should be easy to carry from place to place. Something that is not portable is not a convenient form of money. Pigs, for example, were probably not easily portable.

5. List four characteristics that something should have if it is to be used as money.

_____

_____

6. Explain why money needs to be portable.

_____

_____

Divisible If you go into a store with a $20 bill, you can buy any item that is not more than $20 including tax. If you buy a $1.95 item, the cashier will, in effect, "break apart" your $20 so that he or she can get the $1.95 plus tax out of it. The rest of your $20 will come back to you as change. If you could not "break apart" your $20 bill, anything that you bought would cost the full $20. A form of money that can't be divided into smaller units—or is not **divisible**—is not efficient. That is one reason that wampum was such a convenient form of money. It was easy to divide and easy to carry around.

Stable Why do you think that paper money is printed in such detail? What would happen if you could just write a dollar amount on a slip of paper and call that money? If this were the case, the amount of money in the economy would keep increasing. Everyone would just keep writing amounts on slips of paper. We want to be able to control the money supply. Think about how the law of supply and demand would work. As the supply of money increased, its value would decrease.

For money to be useful, it must be stable. That means that the supply must be controllable so that its value does not change a lot over time. As you learned in Chapter 4, inflation can cause money to lose some of its buying power. **Buying power** is the amount of goods and services that money will purchase. Loss of buying power due to inflation is, however, usually quite slow and steady.

7. Why is it important for money to be divisible?

_____

_____

8. Is it important for the money supply to be controllable? Explain.

_____

_____

✔ Check Your Understanding

The chart below shows some items that have been used as money by past societies. For each item, decide which of the four necessary characteristics of money it has. Write *yes* or *no* in each blank to complete the chart.

	Coconuts	Reindeer	Drums	Shells
Durable?				
Portable?				
Divisible?				
Stable?				

Types of Money

There are three types of money. What makes each type unique is how it gets its value. These types of money are:

- commodity money
- fiat money
- representative money

Commodity Money Money that is valuable in itself is called **commodity money.** Gold is a precious metal, so a gold coin is commodity money. Even if you melted down the coin so that it was no longer money, it would still have value.

Fiat Money Money that is valuable because a government says so is called **fiat money**. A fiat is a government order, so fiat money is valuable by government order. The **currency**—coins and paper money—used in the United States is a form of fiat money. The money itself is only paper or common metal and is of little value. But the government has assigned values to the currency, so that people recognize it as valuable.

Representative Money Money that stands for, or represents, something else of value is called **representative money**. Two forms of representative money that are used today are personal checks and traveler's checks.

Personal checks **Personal checks** represent the money in a person's checking account at a bank. A merchant receiving a check for $20 can cash that check for a $20 bill. Most purchases and debts in this country are paid for with checks. Checks are convenient because they can be written for an exact amount. They are also safer to carry than money because only the person to whom the check is made out can cash it. Checks also require the person's signature.

Traveler's checks **Traveler's checks** represent money that a person has already paid to a large bank or company. Traveler's checks are sold to customers, who in turn use them to pay for goods or services. The banks and companies guarantee payment to the person receiving the traveler's check. Because of this guarantee, traveler's checks are accepted in most places throughout the world. Personal checks, on the other hand, are usually accepted only within the state where the person's bank is located.

9. What are the three types of money?

_____

_____

10. How does commodity money get its value?

_____

_____

11. How does fiat money get its value?

_____

_____

12. What are two forms of representative money?

_____

_____

When Sarah first got her credit cards, she thought of them as a form of money. But are credit cards a form of money?

When you buy a coat and pay for it with cash or a check, you have paid with a form of money. When you use a credit card, you have only promised to pay with money or a check sometime in the future.

Credit cards are not money; they are a promise of payment. Money has, or stores, a certain amount of value. A $10 bill is worth 10 dollars. A check is worth the exact amount written on it. A credit card has no stored value. A merchant cannot use the credit card slip that you signed to buy other goods or services, so credit cards are *not* a form of money.

TAKE ANOTHER LOOK

The chart below has a column for each of the three ways that money stores value. To the left of the columns is a list of different types of money. Put a check mark in the correct column for each type of money shown.

HOW VARIOUS TYPES OF MONEY STORE THEIR VALUE

	COMMODITY MONEY	FIAT MONEY	REPRESENTATIVE MONEY
Traveler's checks			
Silver ingots			
U.S. pennies			
U.S. dollar bills			
Personal checks			

Near Money

Goods that are almost, but not exactly, like money are called **near money**. Savings accounts are an example of near money. A **savings account** is an agreement with a bank. The bank agrees to hold your money and pay you interest on it. You agree to let the bank use your money while it is in your account. The bank pays you interest on your savings account for the temporary loan, or use, of your money. Savings accounts are a store of value, but they are not a medium of exchange. You would have to remove the money from your savings account before you could use it to buy goods.

Two types of savings accounts are **passbook accounts** and **certificates of deposit (CDs)**. You can take your money out, or withdraw it, from a passbook account at any time. Certificates of deposit, on the other hand, are issued for a specific number of months or years. If you withdraw money from a CD early, you must pay an interest penalty.

13. What is near money?

_____

_____

14. Give one example of near money.

_____

_____

15. How do passbook accounts differ from certificates of deposit?

_____

_____

Financial Institutions

Savings and loan associations (S&Ls) and **banks** are two types of financial institutions. Generally, they provide the same services.

Savings and Loan Associations Historically, S&Ls only accepted savings deposits and made loans. In particular, S&Ls made loans to people buying homes. Today S&Ls also offer checking accounts. S&Ls are often smaller institutions than banks.

Banks Like S&Ls, banks accept savings deposits and make loans. Historically, they have provided a wider variety of loans than S&Ls, including business loans. An important function of banks is to provide checking accounts to depositors. Remember, checks are the most widely used form of money in the U.S. economy. Banks are the main holders of the money in checking accounts. Banks generally charge fees for their services.

16. Name two types of financial institutions.

_____

_____

17. What is the most important function of banks?

_____

_____

Both banks and S&Ls pay interest to customers on their savings accounts. Some banks and S&Ls also pay interest on interest-bearing checking accounts. Interest is figured as a percentage of the amount of money in an account. Financial institutions usually pay slightly higher interest rates on savings accounts than they do on checking accounts.

Customers pay interest to banks and S&Ls on their loans. Anyone who takes out a loan pays interest on the money that is borrowed. The interest rates that customers pay on loans are usually higher than the interest rates that institutions pay to depositors. For example, Sarah paid 21 percent interest annually on a bank credit card balance. That rate is not uncommon with credit cards. On the other hand, banks might only pay from 3 to 5 percent on interest-bearing accounts.

18. What is interest?

_____

_____

Money Supply

Banks and S&Ls perform another important economic function. They influence the money supply. The **money supply** is the total value of currency and checkable deposits—including personal and traveler's checks—held by the public. It is the total amount of money in the U.S. economy. How do financial institutions expand the money supply? They do this by loaning money and providing checking accounts.

For example, one morning, Sarah opens a savings account with a $1,000 deposit. That afternoon, Sarah's bank lends $500 of her deposit to Nayan. Nayan immediately puts this loan money into a new checking account so that he can use it when he needs it.

By day's end, the bank has two new accounts with total deposits of $1,000 + $500, or $1,500. They have increased the money supply by $500. The $500 is, in effect, counted twice—once when Sarah deposits it, and again when Nayan deposits it. When loans are made, the money supply increases.

19. What is the money supply?

_____

_____

20. How do financial institutions expand the money supply?

_____

_____

The Federal Reserve System

Control of the U.S. money supply is the responsibility of the Federal Reserve System of the United States, also known as "The Fed." The **Federal Reserve System** is the central banking system of the United States. It has 12 main Federal Reserve Banks and 25 Federal Reserve branch banks. All national commercial banks must be members of the Federal Reserve System. The Fed is supervised by a seven-member Board of Governors appointed by the President and approved by the Senate. The Fed has four main functions:

- overseeing and regulating the U.S. banking system
- supplying currency
- clearing checks
- controlling the U.S. money supply

21. What are the four main functions of The Fed?

_____

_____

_____

_____

Overseeing and Regulating The Fed regularly audits, or examines, the records of banks throughout the country. It also determines the percentage of their deposits that banks must keep on reserve and the percentage that they can loan out.

Supplying Currency The Fed keeps the currency supply fresh by replacing worn-out bills with new ones. For example, the average $1 bill lasts only 18 months before it begins tearing and needs to be replaced. The Fed also issues new currency. It is now in the process of replacing the almost 2 billion $100 bills in circulation with newly designed bills. The new $100 bills will be more difficult to counterfeit.

Clearing Checks Checks that are written against an account at one bank are often cashed at another bank. Sometimes this other bank is in another part of the country. The Fed keeps track of how much money must be taken out from the first bank and transferred to the second bank. Each cashed check, also called a canceled check, is returned to the bank that issued it. Usually, that bank returns it to the customer in a bank statement. A **bank statement** is a record of all the transactions in an account during a month. Look at the back of a canceled check. It should have the stamp of at least one district branch bank of the Federal Reserve System.

Controlling the U.S. Money Supply As you learned in Chapter 4, a money supply that is too large can cause inflation. A money supply that is too small can cause deflation, or slow down the economy. The Fed tries to achieve the right balance between inflation and deflation. It does this in a number of ways.

The Fed can raise or lower the percentage of deposits that banks must keep on reserve. The percentage affects the amount of money that banks and S&Ls can loan and, in turn, the size of the money supply. The Fed can also raise or lower the interest rate that it charges when it loans money to banks. The lower the interest rate, the more money goes out in loans and the larger the money supply becomes.

Finally, The Fed can sell or buy back government bonds. **Government bonds** are notes representing loans that the government promises to repay with interest. When The Fed sells these bonds, it takes the money that it receives out of circulation, which reduces the money supply. When The Fed buys them back, it puts the money back into circulation, which increases the money supply.

22. Why is The Fed concerned with the size of the money supply?

_____

_____

23. List two ways in which The Fed can control the money supply.

_____

_____

Protecting the Consumer

The Fed also helps federal and state legislatures design banking laws that protect consumers. Over the past 30 years, the federal government has passed a number of laws regulating credit and other bank activities.

The first of these laws was the 1968 Truth in Lending Act. This act requires lending institutions to inform borrowers fully about loan details. For example, borrowers must be told precisely what their interest rate and repayment schedule will be before they sign loan papers. They must also be told about all fees that they are expected to pay. The act also protects consumers against being charged for purchases made after a credit card is reported lost or stolen.

In 1974, Congress passed the Equal Credit Opportunity Act. This act guarantees equal access to credit for all people regardless of gender, ethnicity, color, age, marital status, or national origin. The act says that lenders must make decisions on the same basis for all applicants who are in a similar economic condition. They cannot treat certain applicants differently from others.

Finally, the Electronic Funds Transfer Act of 1978 protects consumers in today's age of computerized banking. Among other provisions, it states that consumers are responsible for no more than $50 in losses if someone uses their bank card illegally at an automatic teller machine. To be protected, though, consumers must report their card missing within two days. The act also requires banks to investigate customer complaints about the accuracy of computerized bank statements.

✔ Check Your Understanding

24. Which federal consumer protection law could each of the following people turn to for help?

    a. David's wallet is stolen with his bank card in it. He calls the bank that day and reports the card stolen. Two weeks later, his bank statement shows that someone has illegally withdrawn $1,200 from his account.

    _____

    _____

    b. Nina borrows $2,000 from a bank to buy a used car. When her first payment bill arrives, she discovers that she owes a $75 processing fee. This fee was not described in any of the papers that the bank gave her before she signed for the loan.

    _____

    _____

    c. Tony is 68 years old and owns a barber shop. He goes to his bank to apply for a business loan. The manager says to him, "Someone who's 68 will just retire in a year or two, and then we're out the money." Tony is turned down for the loan. He believes that the rejection was based on his age.

    _____

    _____

USING ECONOMICS SKILLS

Reading a Checking Account Statement

As you learned earlier, a bank statement is a summary of a person's banking activities during one month. Often, bank statements include several accounts. The page below shows one of Sarah's bank statements. It covers her checking account activity for January. Sarah reads through her statement carefully and compares it with her other records, such as her checkbook register and paycheck stubs.

Washtenaw Savings Bank
Customer: Sarah Peters   Checking Acct No.: 7825004
Checking Activity from 01/01/96 to 01/31/96

Post. Date	Transaction	Fees	Trans. Amt.	New Bal.
01/01/96	Check Bal. Forward			$1144.90
01/02/96	Check #0670		26.13-	1118.77
01/04/96	Deposit by check		525.04	1643.81
01/08/96	Withdrawal	0.80-	100.00-	1543.01
01/10/96	Check #0671		10.00-	1533.01
01/10/96	Check #0674		10.00-	1523.01
01/12/96	Check #0673		24.09-	1498.92
01/15/96	Direct Deposit Royce Bros.		802.50	2301.42
01/19/96	Check #0676		32.90-	2268.52
01/20/96	Withdrawal	0.80-	60.00-	2207.72
01/25/96	Check #0675		450.00-	1757.72
01/25/96	Check #0672		110.35-	1647.37
01/30/96	Direct Deposit Royce Bros.		802.50	2449.87
01/31/96	Interest		1.19	2451.06
01/31/96	Ending Balance			2451.06

1. On posting date 1/02/96, does Sarah make a deposit or a withdrawal? for what amount?

_____

2. How does Sarah arrive at a new balance after making a deposit?

_____

3. Sarah's rent is $450. What was the number of the rent check?

_____

4. On 1/19/96, Sarah paid a credit card debt. What was her new balance after the check was paid?

_____

Vocabulary

Complete each sentence with a term from the list below.

The Fed	exchange	commodity money
divisible	barter	money supply
buying power	fiat money	

1. The amount of goods and services that money will purchase is its

   _____.

2. _____ is the trade of goods and services for other goods and services, or for money.

3. _____ is the direct trading of one item or service for another.

4. Money that is valuable because a government says so is called

   _____.

5. Money must be _____, or able to be divided into smaller units.

6. _____ controls the U.S. money supply.

7. _____ is a form of money that is valuable in itself.

8. The _____ is the total value of currency and checkable deposits in the economy.

Main Idea

Answer the following questions.

9. What are four desirable characteristics for an item to be used as money?

   _____   _____

   _____   _____

10. What are three services that banks provide?

    _____

    _____

    _____

Understanding Economics

11. Suppose you work the cash register at a clothing boutique. What types of money could customers use? What form of payment could they use that isn't money?

_____

_____

_____

_____

_____

12. Suppose you have $1,000 that you want to put into a savings account to pay for college. What type of savings account might be best for you? How long will it be before you need to withdraw the money? How will this affect your decision about which type of account to choose?

_____

_____

_____

_____

_____

_____

_____

Project

Find out which bank in your area offers the best services for students. With your class, make a list of what to look for when choosing a bank. You might include such factors as interest rates, minimum required deposit, service charges, and bank location. Then visit local banks to collect brochures and information packets. Make a chart comparing the services offered at each bank. As a group, decide which bank most closely meets your needs.

Lucas Alvarez has a brand new bachelor's degree in computer science, and he's about to put it to work. Nortec, Inc.—the maker of some of the most popular computer games on the market—has hired him. Lucas is thrilled because he's been working on his own computer games at home, and now he has a chance to design more for Nortec.

Lucas wants to get right to work discussing his ideas with all the other designers. However, before he can dive in, there is still a lot of paperwork to do with Mr. Melendez, the personnel manager.

When is the best time to start retirement planning?

Planning for Retirement

During the initial interview, Mr. Melendez told Lucas that Nortec offered "a generous benefits package." Lucas wasn't quite sure, though, just what that claim meant. Mr. Melendez explained that it meant a two-week vacation, health and dental insurance, and a good retirement plan. Mr. Melendez also told Lucas that he had to make some early decisions about his retirement plan. "Retirement?" Lucas asked. "Why would I want to start thinking about retirement now? I have at least 40 good working years to go!"

"This is a perfect time to start," Mr. Melendez said with a smile. He then explained to Lucas why he should start investing money in a retirement plan as soon as possible.

"The government provides Social Security income to retired people," Mr. Melendez began. "But if you depend on Social Security alone, then you won't have nearly enough money to live on. That's why it's important for you to start investing now. You'll be able to accumulate a lot of money through the years. You can add that money to your Social Security benefits and have enough money for your retirement."

Lucas Alvarez listens as Nortec's personnel manager explains retirement options.

Lucas was smart when it came to computers, but he was realizing that he didn't know much about investing money. Previously when he had heard the word *investments*, he had thought about the future—about 20 years down the road. After listening to Mr. Melendez, Lucas was beginning to realize that the future is now.

It All Adds Up

"Starting to invest when you're 22 years old makes a big difference," Mr. Melendez told Lucas. "Don't wait until you're 42."

"Because if I save for 40 years, then I'll have twice as much as if I saved for 20 years, right?" Lucas asked.

Mr. Melendez smiled and shook his head. "Actually, you'll have much more than twice as much," he said. "There is a formula that investment counselors use to figure out how much money an investment will accumulate over a certain period of time. For example, if you save just $50 a month at 10 percent interest a year and the interest is compounded monthly, you'll have $10,327.60 after 10 years. After 20 years, you'll have $38,284.85. After 30 years, you'll have $113,966.27."

Lucas was surprised. "Would it really be that much?" he asked.

"Yes. It happens if the returns on your investment are all reinvested," Mr. Melendez explained.

Lucas realized exactly what he should do. "OK," he said, "I'm going to start investing in myself right away."

Matching Dollar for Dollar

"Great," Mr. Melendez said. "Fifty dollars will be deducted from your paycheck every month. That's about $25 every two weeks. Nortec will match your contributions. For every dollar you invest, we'll invest another dollar for you. That means that you'll be investing $100 a month. Now, let's take a look at the mutual funds in which you can invest."

"What's a mutual fund?" Lucas asked.

"A mutual fund is a company that pools together people's investment monies and then invests that pooled money in various stocks and bonds," Mr. Melendez said. "Some mutual funds invest primarily in stocks. Others invest mainly in bonds. Some invest in both. Investing in a mutual fund may be safer than buying individual stocks and bonds. You're not putting all your eggs in one basket. Which type would you like?"

"Well, I'm not sure that I understand," Lucas said. "What's the difference between stocks and bonds?"

Assessing the Risk

"Bonds are loans of a sort," Mr. Melendez explained. "When you buy a bond, you lend money to a business or corporation or to a government—maybe to the federal government or maybe to a city government. It is strictly a loan on which you will earn interest. When you buy stock, you own part of a corporation. If the value of the corporation goes up, then the value of the stock usually goes up, too. You earn money by receiving dividends, a small part of the company's profits, or by selling the stock for a profit."

"Which are better, stocks or bonds?" Lucas asked.

"That depends, in part, on how much risk you want to take," Mr. Melendez said. "Bonds are safer, but on average, they don't earn as much as stocks. Stocks may earn more, but they are riskier. However, over time, the stock market may be a

The fast pace of the Boston Stock Exchange is typical of all stock markets. Stock exchanges are marketplaces where stocks are bought and sold.

smarter investment for you because it has a higher average return—about 10 percent a year.

"Investment counselors often suggest that young people go with stocks," Mr. Melendez added. "This investment may make sense because the longer you have until retirement, the more opportunities you have to make up any losses associated with stocks. If retirement is just around the corner, then you may be safer with bonds."

Lucas took a deep breath. He'd never dreamed that he'd have to make decisions in his 20s that would affect him 40 years down the road. But he knew exactly what he wanted to do. "I'll go for a stock mutual fund," he told Mr. Melendez.

As Lucas left the personnel department, he decided to start checking out some stocks on his own. He said to himself: "What do I have to lose? I'm young and can take a few risks."

Lucas has made some wise decisions as he starts his job at Nortec. By taking out money from each paycheck and investing in himself first, Lucas is investing in his future.

Stocks and Bonds

Like Lucas, more and more young people are investing in themselves. They are also investing in companies that make products they are familiar with. For example, food, clothing, computer software, and movie companies are all high on the investment lists of young people getting a head start on the future. These young investors aren't just making money, they're also getting a good education in personal finances.

Starting an Investment Program

An **investment**, in terms of personal finance, is the act of using money to get back something in return—namely a profit—in the future. For example, when Lucas decided to invest in a mutual fund, he did so because he wanted to make a profit on the money that he invested. When people make investments, they may invest in various types of securities. **Securities** are stocks and bonds.

The type of security in which Lucas decided to invest is called a stock mutual fund. A **mutual fund** is a company that pools together the investment monies of many people and then invests those monies in stocks and bonds.

1. Why do investors buy stocks and bonds?

_____

_____

_____

Every day, millions of people decide to invest their money in securities for many reasons. They might want to buy a boat or a house in five years. They may want to get started on saving for their child's education or for their own retirement. Before any investments can be made, it's important to look at the choices available when buying securities. Here's a look at some of the securities in which people can invest:

- bonds
    - savings bonds
- mutual funds
    - general mutual funds
    - sector mutual funds

- stocks
  - common stocks
  - preferred stocks

2. Name three investment options.

_____

_____

3. What are two types of stock?

_____

_____

Bonds

As you learned in Chapter 5, a bond is an interest-bearing certificate issued by a corporation or a government. In return for the use of the investor's money, the corporation or government promises to pay the investor a certain amount of interest over a certain period of time. The corporation or government also promises to return the money that it borrowed when that period ends.

U.S. Savings Bonds A popular type of bond is the U.S. Savings Bond. These federal government bonds are sold at banks and other financial institutions. Some employers also have plans that automatically take money from an employee's paycheck to buy savings bonds.

A savings bond has a specific face value. When you buy the bond, you pay less than its face value. For example, when you buy a $50 bond, you may pay only $25. When you cash in your bond, you get back the bond's full face value, which reflects the interest earned. On a 20-year $100 bond, you, or someone you've sold the bond to, waits 20 years before collecting the $100. Remember, though, that you may have paid only $50 for the bond originally. The difference reflects the interest earned.

4. What is a bond?

_____

_____

5. What accounts for the difference between the amount paid for a bond and the face value of the bond?

_____

6. How long would someone have to wait to get the full face value of a 20-year savings bond?

_____

_____

The Advantage of Bonds The great advantage of government bonds—including U.S. Savings Bonds—is that they are very safe investments. There is little risk, unless inflation is a problem. The amount of risk on an investment refers to the chance that it has of making or losing a large amount of money. The higher the risk, the greater the chance that the investment will do very well or very poorly. Government bonds are low-risk investments. For example, U.S. Savings Bonds are backed by the U.S. government. That means the federal government guarantees that you will get the money you expect to get. People who don't want to risk losing any of their money often invest in U.S. Savings Bonds.

The Disadvantages of Bonds The main disadvantage of bonds is that they often don't provide as much profit, or return, as some higher-risk investments. Generally, bonds are more profitable than savings accounts at banks, but they are often less profitable than stocks.

7. What is a big advantage of investing in government bonds?

_____

_____

8. What is the major disadvantage of investing in bonds?

_____

_____

Stocks

You also learned in Chapter 5 that buying a share of stock is buying partial ownership of a business. When a business needs to raise money, it can sell shares of company stock. People who own shares of stock in a corporation are called stockholders.

Stockholders may make money from their stock shares in two ways. One way is to speculate. **Speculation** is the practice of engaging in business transactions with a high risk factor in the hope of making large amounts of money. When stockholders speculate, they buy stock, hoping that its price per share will increase. If the price of the stock goes up, then the stockholder can sell the stock to make a profit. Profits made from the sale or trading of an investment, such as stock shares, are called **capital gains**.

The other way stockholders can make money is through dividends. In Chapter 5, you learned that a dividend is money that a corporation may pay on each share of its stock. Corporations usually only pay stockholders dividends when they have made a profit. On the other hand, there are corporations that never pay dividends. Instead, their profits are reinvested in that corporation.

Types of Stocks

There are two main categories of stocks. Most stockholders own shares of common stock; a small number of stockholders hold shares of preferred stock. **Preferred stocks** guarantee their stockholders dividends, but these stockholders have no voting rights in the corporation. **Common stocks** may pay dividends, but do not guarantee to do so; these stockholders have voting rights.

9. What are two ways that stockholders can make money on their investments?

_____

_____

10. What are capital gains?

_____

_____

11. How does preferred stock differ from common stock?

_____

_____

The Disadvantage of Stocks

If a corporation does not do well, then the price of its stock might fall. If a stockholder sells when the price of the stock is down, then the stockholder may lose some of the original money that he or she invested. This loss of investment is called a **capital loss**. It is one of the disadvantages of higher-risk investments like stocks.

The Advantage of Stocks

While the risk with stocks is greater than with bonds, the potential gains are greater, too. Stocks often make more money over a 10- to 20-year period for an investor than do bonds. Stocks historically return about 10 percent a year on an investment.

When the price of a stock rises a great deal, a company may declare a stock split. A **stock split** gives shareholders two or more shares of stock for every one share they own. If it's a two-for-one split, then the price of each share of stock would fall to about one-half of its pre-split value. So, the number of shares that a stockholder owns doubles, but the total value of those shares stays about the same.

Companies split stocks to keep down the price of each share of stock. For example, suppose Lucas owns 50 shares of Nortec stock. The current value for Nortec stock is $100 per share. Nortec decides to split its stock and give stockholders two shares for every one share they own. This means that Lucas now owns 100 shares of Nortec stock and each share is now probably worth $50.

12. What are capital losses?

_____

_____

13. Explain what happens when a stock splits.

_____

_____

Buying and Selling Stocks

The buying and selling of stocks and bonds is done by people known as brokers. A **broker** acts as a middle person between a buyer and a seller. Brokers work at brokerage firms across the country, where they buy and sell stocks and bonds for individuals and groups.

For example, suppose Lucas wants to buy more shares of Nortec stock. He would call J. Williams & Company, the brokerage firm that handled his first purchase of Nortec stock, and talk with his broker, Anna Chung. Anna would then call one of J. Williams & Company's brokers on the floor of the stock exchange and put in an order to buy a certain number of shares of Nortec stock.

Stock exchanges are marketplaces where stocks are bought and sold. Stock exchanges list only those stocks that they have approved for trade. Some of the biggest stock exchanges are the New York Stock Exchange; the American Stock Exchange; and NASDAQ, which stands for the National Association of Securities Dealers Automated Quotation. NASDAQ is an electronic exchange; its computer center is in Trumbull, Connecticut. All trading for NASDAQ is done electronically on computers. Keep in mind that stock exchanges only provide a place where stocks can be bought and sold.

After buying the Nortec stock, Anna would inform Lucas that he had bought the extra shares of Nortec at the market price. J. Williams & Company would then hold those shares in Lucas' account. For each stock purchase, a stock certificate is issued.

14. Where are shares of stock bought and sold?

_____

_____

_____

15. What is the function of a broker?

_____

_____

_____

16. Describe the step that Lucas needs to take to buy shares of Nortec stock?

_____

_____

_____

✔ *Check Your Understanding*

Use the chart below to compare stocks and bonds. Then answer the questions that follow.

BONDS VS. STOCKS		
	Advantage	Disadvantage
Bonds	often less risk	often lower return
Stocks	chance for higher return	often more risk

17. What is the advantage of bonds? What is their disadvantage?

_____

_____

18. What is the advantage of stocks? What is their disadvantage?

_____

_____

Mutual Funds

When Lucas talked to Mr. Melendez, he asked what type of mutual fund Lucas preferred. He said that some of the company's mutual funds invested in bonds, some invested in stocks, and some invested in both.

As you know, a mutual fund is a company that pools together the investment monies of many people and then invests those monies in stocks or bonds or both. Mutual fund companies are often able to invest more skillfully and more economically than individual investors.

These companies follow the markets daily and have research departments to keep track of the latest developments in the business world. As a result, a mutual fund often provides investors with a higher rate of return than they could probably make on their own.

19. What is a mutual fund?

_____

_____

TAKE ANOTHER LOOK

Read the title to see what information the chart below shows. Then answer the question that follows.

BENEFITS OF INVESTING IN A MUTUAL FUND

Compared to buying stocks and bonds on your own, a mutual fund can:

- lower your risk by spreading it out among many stocks and bonds.
- lower your expenses by buying/selling stocks and bonds in large quantities at discounted fees.
- increase your investments' earnings by skillfully buying at low prices and selling at high prices, based on expert research and experience.

---

20. What are some of the benefits of investing through a mutual fund rather than investing on your own in individual stocks and bonds?

_____

_____

_____

Types of Mutual Funds

Each mutual fund has its own investment strategy. Some low-risk funds invest only in bonds. Some higher-risk funds invest almost exclusively in stocks. Some try to balance the risk of stocks with the safety of bonds by investing in both.

Mutual funds also differ from one another in their choice of stocks. **General mutual funds** include securities from diverse business sectors, such as McDonald's, AT&T, and The Home Depot. On the other hand, **sector mutual funds** include securities in a particular business sector, such as Apple Computer, Intel, and IBM in the technology sector.

21. What is the difference between a general mutual fund and a sector mutual fund?

_____

_____

_____

Investing in Mutual Funds

Before making any investment decisions, there are quite a few important questions that you should ask yourself. By thoughtfully answering these questions, you can make smart investment choices with which you are comfortable. First, it's important to decide whether you want to invest in mutual funds or individual securities or a combination of both. If you are thinking of investing in mutual funds, then you should ask yourself these questions:

- **Do you want to invest in a general mutual fund or a sector mutual fund?** There is less risk with general mutual funds than with sector mutual funds.

- **Do you want a fund that charges sales fees or a fund that does not?** Sales fees can end up cutting into your profits. For example, specialized sector funds, such as technology funds, are considered high-risk and may have a sales fee.

- **Do you want a high-risk fund that has the chance to grow at a good rate? Or do you want a low-risk fund?** Low-risk funds may grow more slowly, but at least you won't have to worry about losing money.

- **Do you want to choose a small-company fund or a big-company fund?** Again, this decision rests on the level of risk with which you are comfortable. A small-company fund is higher risk than a big-company fund.

- **Who is managing the fund?** Many people say that the manager's record and experience are the most important factor to consider when choosing a mutual fund. Finance magazines and books provide information on how various funds and managers have performed over time.

22. Which types of mutual funds might be a good choice for a person who doesn't like to take big risks? Explain.

_____

_____

23. What do some people think is critical in choosing the best mutual fund?

_____

_____

TAKE ANOTHER LOOK

Look at the chart below. It shows some of the stocks that a mutual fund company purchased on a certain day for one of its general funds. The stocks are shown by sector. To understand what the chart shows, read the titles for each column.

NEW AMERICA MUTUAL FUND		
SECTOR AND STOCK	**SHARES**	**$ VALUE** (10/27/95)
Athletic Footwear		
Converse	35,000	166,250
Nike(b)	20,000	2,237,500
Reebok	25,000	856,250
General Apparel		
Benetton	50,000	1,025,000
Gap, Inc.	15,000	562,500
The Limited	30,000	588,750
Urban Outfitters	40,000	880,000
Retail, Specialty		
Bed, Bath, & Beyond	25,000	759,375
Pier 1 Imports	15,000	142,500

24. Which sectors are shown in this chart?

_____

_____

25. What is New America's most valuable stock holding?

_____

If you are thinking about investing in individual stocks, then ask yourself these questions:

- **What is your objective? Do you want to make a long-term or short-term investment?** For example, if you decide that you want to use the money that you make from your investments to buy a house in 3 years, then that would be a short-term investment. If you want to use the money that you make from your investments for your retirement and you are only 18 years old, then that would be a long-term investment.

- **Do you have a tolerance for high-risks or only for low-risks?** Young people usually have a higher risk tolerance because they normally will not need to use the money that they make from their investments for a long time.

- **How much time do you want to spend on your investments?** Researching stocks and following the stock market takes time. If you're interested, though, you'll enjoy it.

Netscape is a company that creates computer software. Before buying the stock, Lucas looked at the company's annual report to answer these questions: Does the company have a lot of debt? Have its sales been steady or increasing over recent years? Have its earnings been growing steadily?

After being satisfied that Netscape's debt was low and that its sales and earnings had been steadily increasing, Lucas decided to buy 20 shares of Netscape.

26. Why did Lucas want to read Netscape's annual report?

_____

_____

The **Dow Jones Industrial Average** records the average performance of a large group of selected industrial stocks. This average gives some sense of how stocks in the industrial sector are doing. It also gives some indication of how the stock market as a whole is doing.

Lucas keeps a notebook in which he records his Netscape stock's performance week after week. He can compare this stock's performance to the performance of the stock market as a whole. Lucas has learned to be careful during a bear market. A **bear market** is a period of generally declining stock prices. He has also learned to enjoy a bull market. A **bull market** is a period of generally increasing stock prices.

27. What is the Dow Jones Industrial Average?

_____

28. During which type of market would most stocks increase in value: a bear market or a bull market?

_____

Think About It!

A week after Lucas buys Netscape, he looks at the following stock listing for Netscape in the newspaper, shown as _NetscCm_. This listing is from the NASDAQ exchange for Friday, October 27, 1995. Notice that the stock prices are listed using fractions. These prices represent dollars and fractions of a dollar (1/8 dollar = $0.125).

STOCK LISTING FOR NETSCAPE (10/27/95)

52-week		Stock	Div.	Sales 100s	High	Low	Last	Change
High	Low							
88	$45^{3/4}$	NetsCm	. . .	5143	$84^{1/2}$	$79^{3/4}$	$81^{1/2}$	$-3^{1/4}$

29. The first two columns show the high and low price for the previous year. What was Netscape's high price during the previous year?

_____

30. "Div." stands for the annual dividend that a company pays on each share of its stock. Did Netscape pay a dividend last year?

_____

31. The column marked "Change" indicates how much money each share gained or lost on the previous business day. What was the change for each share of Netscape stock on the previous business day? Was it a gain or a loss?

_____

32. The column marked "Last" indicates a stock's closing price for the previous business day. Lucas bought his shares when the stock was at $79^{1}/_{2}$. Has each share gained or lost value in the week since Lucas bought this stock? How much?

_____

Investing in Yourself

In addition to the money that is taken out of his paycheck for the mutual fund at work, Lucas has decided to take another $50 from each paycheck and deposit it in a money market mutual fund. A **money market mutual fund** is a mutual fund that invests in money market certificates. It is a savings account in which you can save money and more interest than on a regular savings or checking account.

Lucas uses his money market mutual fund to save money to buy stocks. When he's saved a certain amount, he then makes a stock purchase. You could use a money market mutual fund to save money for a car or just to save money.

TAKE ANOTHER LOOK

A circle graph is a good way to compare information. The two circle graphs below show recommended investment strategies for a 25 year old and a 45 year old. The percentages represent how much of each investment portfolio should be in each type of fund. Financial counselors usually suggest higher-risk investments for younger people and lower-risk investments for older people.

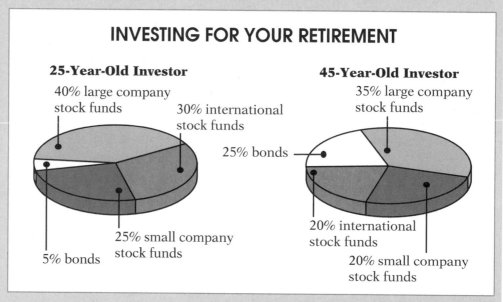

INVESTING FOR YOUR RETIREMENT

25-Year-Old Investor
40% large company stock funds
30% international stock funds
25% small company stock funds
5% bonds

45-Year-Old Investor
35% large company stock funds
25% bonds
20% international stock funds
20% small company stock funds

33. What is the biggest difference between the two investment strategies? Explain.

_____

_____

Reading a Double-Line Graph

A double-line graph allows you to compare two sets of data quickly. The double-line graph below shows the high/low stock prices for one share of common stock between 1990 and 1995.

STOCK PRICE HISTORY: GAP, INC.

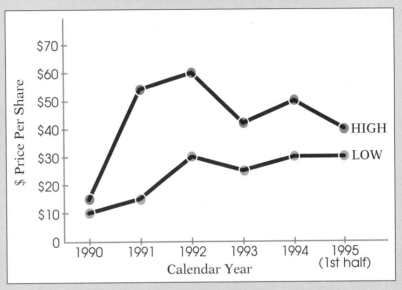

Read the graph title and labels to find out what information is on the double-line graph. Now, suppose you want to find out what the high and low prices for one share of Gap, Inc., stock were in 1990. First, find 1990 on the bottom of the graph. Then move up above that year until you reach the dot for the low. Then move to the left to find the price for that year. The low price for Gap, Inc., stock in 1990 was $10. Repeat these steps for the high. The high price for Gap, Inc., stock in 1990 was about $17.

Use the graph to answer the following questions.

1. What was the highest price for Gap, Inc., stock during the period shown?

_____

2. Between which two years did the price per share fall?

_____

3. In which year was there the greatest difference between the high and the low?

_____

Vocabulary

Complete each sentence with a term from the list below.

bull market	mutual fund	preferred stock
stock split	bear market	capital gains
speculation	stock exchanges	

1. _____ is the practice of investing in high-risk transactions in the hope of making large profits.

2. _____ are marketplaces where stocks are bought and sold.

3. Shares of _____ always promise to pay dividends, but the stockholders have no voting rights.

4. A _____ gives shareholders two or more shares of stock for every one share that they own.

5. A _____ describes a period of generally declining stock prices.

6. _____ are profits earned from the sale or trading of an investment, such as stock shares.

7. A _____ is a company that invests the pooled monies of many people.

8. A _____ describes a period of generally increasing stock prices.

Main Idea

Answer the following questions.

9. Why is it important to begin investing at a young age?

_____

_____

_____

_____

10. What are two types of investments?

_____

_____

11. Why might an investor choose to invest in bonds rather than stocks?

_____

_____

Understanding Economics

12. Suppose you have $1,000 that you want to invest. What would you do differently if you were investing it to help pay for college rather than for retirement?

_____

_____

13. Suppose you have another $1,000 to invest. Think about a company in which you'd like to invest. It may be a company from which you buy products, such as snack foods, athletic shoes, or clothing. Or it may be a company for which you or someone you know works. Explain why you think the company would be a good investment. Remember that your goal as an investor is to make money.

_____

_____

_____

Project

With your classmates, choose two stocks to investigate. Find out as much information as possible about each stock. Where is the stock traded? How much does a share cost? You might also call or write the investor relations departments of the companies. They are usually happy to send out annual reports and other current information. After you've gathered the information, decide which stock would be the better investment. Then follow the progress of the stocks. Was your choice the most profitable one?

It was the end of Max Garcia's junior year in high school, and Max needed a summer job. He had looked everywhere, but it seemed as if all the jobs were taken.

Max talked to his best friend, Jenny, about his dilemma. She suggested that he call her uncle. Jenny's uncle is a carpenter, and he needed an assistant. Max called Mr. Smalls and before he knew it, he had the job. Max was relieved. One of the reasons he needed a job right away was so that he could afford a great present for Jenny's 16th birthday.

Max knew what he wanted to get Jenny—a portable cassette player. She loved music and would really like being able to listen to it all the time. Now Max had only three questions: Which portable cassette player should he buy? Where should he buy it? How much should he pay for it?

Asking the Right Questions

Max asked his sister Lucy where to shop. "Go to Giant Electronics," Lucy said. "They have everything." So Max took the city bus to Giant Electronics one evening. It was a huge place. It had a computer department, a

Is there a smart way to shop?

large camera department, and a television department, as well as a video department. It took Max about half an hour to find the stereos because he kept stopping to look in the various departments.

A salesperson showed Max the portable cassette players. The display case showed six different players. The most expensive player cost $125. It was a Superspin. The least expensive player cost $19. It was a B-Line.

"Which one do you want?" the salesperson asked Max.

"I'm not sure," Max said. "Can you tell me about them?"

Talking to friends about products that you like and why is just one way of becoming a well-informed consumer.

"They're all pretty much the same," the salesperson said. "If I were you, I'd buy this model for $125."

"Why should I spend $125 if all the players are about the same?" Max asked.

"Well," the salesperson said. "Superspin is a really good brand. A lot of people buy this one. Do you want the player or not?"

"I guess not. Not today," Max said. He left the store.

Shopping Around

Max was confused. Should he go back and buy the Superspin? The cost of the Superspin was a lot more than he'd planned to spend. He'd have to really budget his money to be able to afford that player by Jenny's birthday.

As Max walked down Main Street, he spotted George's Radio Shop. Max walked into the store and was greeted by George himself.

"May I help you?" George asked. Max told him that he wanted to buy a personal

Smart shopping means comparing prices, features, and warranties of different products and brands before spending your money.

cassette player. "How much do you want to spend?" George asked.

"About $30," Max said.

"That's a reasonable price," George said. "You can get a good player for $30. What features do you want?"

"I'm not sure," Max said.

George described some typical portable player features. The basic choice was between a machine that was just a tape player, and a machine that also had a radio. From there, the choices were dizzying. Max could get digital tuning, pre-set tuning, fast forward and rewind controls, tape rewind, auto-reverse, automatic stop, a bass booster, a graphic equalizer, noise suppression, and more. On top of all that, he could either get a sports model or a regular model.

"Too many choices," Max said. "I'm confused."

"Here," George said. He gave Max a copy of an article about personal cassette players in a consumer magazine. "Take this home and read it. Then come back when you're ready to make a decision."

Making a Smart Decision

Max brought the article home. He learned just about everything that he needed to know about personal tape players. After reading carefully, he decided that he wanted a machine with both a radio and a tape player.

He also decided that the player should have both digital and pre-set tuning and have auto-reverse, fast forward, and rewind controls.

Digital tuning lets the user tune in radio stations precisely on an LCD display. Preset buttons would let Jenny choose her favorite stations and move directly from one station to another. Auto-reverse automatically plays the other side of the tape when it finishes on one side.

The other features didn't matter so much to Max. Almost all the players had automatic tape forward and rewind. Automatic stop prevented the player from running out of battery power. Max didn't care much about a bass booster, graphic equalizer, or noise suppression. These were features that were supposed to improve a player's sound. In the magazine article, Max read that most of the better models came with these features anyway.

Getting the Most for Your Money

The magazine article also indicated which models were the best values. Max had decided that he didn't want a sports model, so he looked at the magazine's rankings of regular models. It showed that the CircleSound player was a very good deal. It had all the features that Max wanted, and its price was between $40 and $50.

Still, $40 or $50 was more than Max wanted to pay. So, he decided that he'd go back to George's tomorrow, take a look at the CircleSound, and ask a few more questions. But that evening, Max saw a big ad for Giant Electronics in the newspaper. The ad read: GIANT SALE! TODAY ONLY. GIANT DISCOUNTS ON EVERYTHING.

Smart shopping pays off. Jenny enjoys her portable cassette player, and Max saves some hard-earned cash.

	PRICE ($)	WEIGHT (OUNCES)	FREQUENCY RESPONSE	FEATURES: RADIO	FEATURES: TAPE
SUPERSPIN	125	11	A	A	A
B-LINE	19	9	F	F	U
CIRCLESOUND	42	10	B	B	C
CLASSIC	35	10	A	B	B

Max thought about the situation. George had certainly been more helpful than the salesperson at Giant Electronics. In fact, he'd not only been more helpful, he'd been much nicer than the salesperson at Giant Electronics, too. On the other hand, Giant's prices seemed lower than George's. What was wrong with going to the place that had the lowest prices?

"Nothing," Lucy told him. "Go to Giant."

Buyer Beware

So Max went to Giant the next day after work. He waited in line for a salesperson. While he waited, Max saw one customer buy a mini-TV. The television that the customer wanted cost $150 on sale. The salesperson said that the store was out of the $150 model. Instead, the customer could buy a different model for $189. Then the salesperson convinced the customer to spend another $18 for batteries and $20 for an extended service contract that would take care of repairs if the television broke.

The next customer wanted to take back a CD system. He'd gotten the wrong system and wanted his money back. "Sorry," the salesperson said. "All sales are final. The best I can do is an exchange. But I'll need to charge you $30 for a restocking fee."

"A restocking fee?" thought Max. He'd never heard of that. It was a charge for returning merchandise. The very next customer had a broken remote control unit. She wanted it replaced under the product's warranty.

"Sorry," said the salesperson. "We don't honor that warranty. You'll have to send it back to the factory."

"Send it back!" Max thought. He'd heard enough. The prices at Giant Electronics were low, but he did not want to deal with extra charges, extended service contracts, restocking fees, and mailing products back for serving. He left the store and walked down to George's Radio.

"How much do you charge for a CircleSound?" Max asked George. George's price was $49.95. At Giant, a CircleSound cost $41.95, but George didn't charge for batteries—and his products had a full 90-day store guarantee. If something went wrong during that time, Max could get his money back with no questions asked.

"What about restocking fees and extended service contracts?" Max asked.

George laughed. His shop didn't have policies like that. George stood behind his products. If something went wrong, George would fix it. But what about price? Max still thought that the CircleSound was out of his price range.

"Have you looked at the Classic?" George asked. Max hadn't. It was the same player as the CircleSound except that it didn't have the bass booster or the graphic equalizer, two features that Max had already decided that he didn't need. The price of the Classic was $34.99.

"Thirty-four ninety-nine!" Max said excitedly. "I'll take it!"

Luxuries vs. Necessities

When Max bought the cassette player, he became a consumer. You'll recall from Chapter 1 that consumers are people who buy goods and services to satisfy their wants and needs. Every time you buy potato chips, clothes, or music, you are a consumer.

As a consumer, you constantly have to make choices. For example, at first Max thought that he could just walk into Giant Electronics and buy a cassette player. He soon found out that there were many decisions involved.

1. Name some items that you buy as a consumer.

_____

_____

_____

What Consumers Buy

The pie chart below shows how typical consumers spend their money. Some of the items on the chart are necessities. **Necessities** are those items that are really needed. Other items on the chart are non-necessities. **Non-necessities**, or **luxuries**, are those items that are not needed but are wanted. Recreation, for example, is something on which you may or may not choose to spend money.

TYPICAL CONSUMER SPENDING

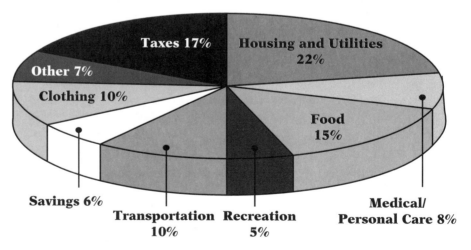

Taxes 17%
Housing and Utilities 22%
Other 7%
Clothing 10%
Food 15%
Savings 6%
Transportation 10%
Recreation 5%
Medical/Personal Care 8%

2. In addition to housing and food, which other items on the pie chart are necessities?

_____

_____

3. With the exception of recreation, which other items on the chart are non-necessities?

_____

_____

4. Suppose you wanted to save money. On which necessities could you reduce your spending most easily? Explain.

_____

_____

Buying: Deciding Whether to Buy

As a consumer, you know that you need to make decisions. You probably see items for sale every day that catch your eye, but you know that you can't buy all of them. How do you decide whether to buy an item? One way is to ask yourself two questions:

- Do I need this item?
- Can I afford this item?

In some cases, your decision will be very clear. If you answer "No" to both questions, it would probably be best if you did not purchase the item that you are considering. If you answer "Yes" to both questions, it probably makes sense to purchase the item that you are considering.

If you answer one "Yes" and one "No," then your decision to buy or not to buy can be tricky. For example, you may think that you _need_ a new coat. But buying a new coat is a mistake if it means that you can't pay your rent. Similarly, you may be able to _afford_ a new pair of expensive boots, but are they really something that you _need_? Could you just as well do without them?

5. When is your decision to buy clear?

_____

_____

6. When is your decision to buy less clear?

_____

_____

Use the chart below to review how to make buying decisions.

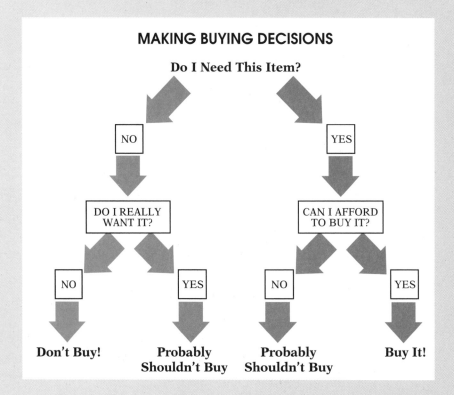

MAKING BUYING DECISIONS

Do I Need This Item?

NO

YES

DO I REALLY
WANT IT?

CAN I AFFORD
TO BUY IT?

NO

YES

NO

YES

Don't Buy!

**Probably
Shouldn't Buy**

**Probably
Shouldn't Buy**

Buy It!

Start at the top of the chart. Ask yourself, "Do I need this?" If your answer is "No," take the path on the left. If your answer is "Yes," take the path on the right. Follow the arrows for each choice. You should end up at one of two choices: "Buy" or "Don't Buy."

7. Suppose you want to buy new athletic shoes. Describe the path that you would take to make this decision.

_____

_____

8. Suppose you want to buy a slice of pizza. Describe the path that you would take to make this decision.

_____

_____

9. Suppose you want to buy a birthday present for a friend. Describe the path that you would take to make this decision.

_____

_____

Making a Budget

One way to make sure that your necessities are paid for is to have a budget. A **budget** is a plan for spending money over a specific period of time. People usually make up budgets based on how often they are paid.

If you are paid weekly, it would make sense to prepare a weekly budget. If you are paid semi-monthly, or twice a month, you would probably want a semi-monthly budget. A budget can help you make decisions about buying items that you may want but that are not necessities. For example, when Max decided that he wanted to buy Jenny a cassette player, he made a budget so that he would have enough money when it came time to make the purchase.

Following is the weekly budget that Max created. It is based on Max's take-home pay, which is $125 a week.

MAX'S WEEKLY BUDGET	
Budget Item	Amount
Carfare	$ 20
Lunch	$ 20
Clothes	$ 25
Recreation	$ 20
Savings	$ 40
TOTAL	$ 125

10. How much does Max spend on recreation?

_____

11. Explain several ways that Max could rework his budget to save money for Jenny's birthday present?

_____

_____

_____

Being an Informed Consumer

Once you've decided what you want to buy, it's time to gather information. There are several ways to gather information.

Friends You can ask your friends which personal cassette players they like and why. Such word-of-mouth opinions can be useful.

Observation You can keep your eye out for cassette players everywhere. You can observe joggers, bicyclists, and people on the bus—anyone you can find using a portable player. You can even ask someone about his or her player if the opportunity arises.

Advertisements You can look at advertisements in your local newspaper. With a quick glance, you'll be able to see the features and prices of various cassette players.

Consumer Publications You can also look at consumer magazines. Consumer magazines are published specifically to give consumers accurate and complete information about products. In addition to consumer magazines, there are also government publications that give information about certain products.

Salespeople Salespeople are usually well informed about the products that they sell. You must keep in mind, however, that they may have their own reasons for wanting you to buy a particular product.

12. When buying a product, which source would you try first? Why?

_____

_____

13. Which sources do you consider the most reliable for information about products? Why?

_____

_____

Comparison Shopping

Once you've gathered information about a product, it's time to do some comparison shopping. Comparing prices on the same product at two or more stores is called **comparison shopping**. For example, Max went to Giant Electronics and George's Radio Shop and found two different prices for a cassette player that he wanted. In general, the more comparison shopping that you do, the better the price you'll get. For best results when comparison shopping, follow these steps:

- Gather information from ads and consumer magazines.
- Go to as many stores as possible: large discount stores, specialty stores, neighborhood stores.
- Compare various brand names, models, and price ranges.
- Compare warranties, guarantees, and service plans.

You might want to keep notes on what you find while comparison shopping. How much comparison shopping you do is up to you. Keep in mind that you should do enough to make an informed decision, but not so much that the comparison shopping itself begins to take too much time and costs too much money.

14. What is comparison shopping?

_____

_____

15. Describe how you would comparison shop if you were buying a new computer.

_____

_____

Buying: Which One?

After deciding that you can afford a purchase, there are still other considerations. For example, once Max decided that he needed and wanted to buy a cassette player for Jenny, he had to ask himself several other questions:

What type of cassette player? A portable cassette player or a portable am/fm stereo cassette player?

What brand? Superspin? CircleSound? Classic? B-Line?

What price? Expensive or inexpensive? $125, $49.95, $41.95, $34.99 or $19?

What features? Do I want a sports model or a regular model? Do I want digital tuning, pre-set tuning, fast forward and rewind controls, tape rewind, auto-reverse, automatic stop, a bass booster, a graphic equalizer, and/or noise suppression?

16. What were some factors that helped Max to make his decision about which cassette player to buy?

_____

_____

17. How is comparison shopping similar to doing homework?

_____

_____

18. What might have happened if Max hadn't comparison shopped?

_____

_____

Consumer Rights

For many years, business owners lived by the slogan, "Let the buyer beware." This slogan means that if products break, don't work right, don't last, or even endanger lives, consumers have no protection.

In 1962, President John F. Kennedy outlined a bill of rights for consumers. **Consumer rights** help protect people against loss or harm from products. Following are the five basic consumer rights that all consumers should expect when they buy a product:

- **Safety**— the right to a safe product
- **Information**— the right to know what a product is and how it is made
- **Choice**— the right to an open market for a product
- **Hearing**— the right to have complaints heard in court
- **Repayment**— the right to payment for harm caused by a product

Of course, the best protection that consumers have is the marketplace itself. When there is competition, a store that tries to sell faulty or harmful products does not usually survive for long. Once the word gets out, people will stop buying from that store and it will go out of business. Consumer rights help protect people against harm from these products. In rare cases, however, even good businesses can sell poor or harmful products.

19. Why do consumers need rights?

_____

_____

20. What five rights do consumers have?

_____   _____

_____   _____

_____

Consumer Complaints: Taking Action

Suppose you go to Honest Al's Electronics to buy a Z-100 laptop computer. It was advertised for $1,100, which is a very low price. But when you ask for a Z-100, the salesperson tells you, "We're all sold out of Z-100s. Anyway, they're not very good. What you want is a Z-200."

The Z-200 costs $1,900, more than you wanted to spend. You buy it anyway. At home, you find that the screen flickers. You bring it back to Honest Al's. The salesperson says, "Sorry, all sales are final. If you want an exchange, you must pay a $50 restocking fee."

You heard this story before when Max went to buy the cassette player at Giant Electronics. Max avoided the situation by buying the player from George's Radio Shop. What should you do if you buy a product from a place like Honest Al's and something goes wrong?

- **Decide:** Make a decision about what you want. Do you want your money back, an exchange, or a repair?
- **Learn:** Find out what the store's policy is for taking back the product. Read store and product information.
- **Gather:** Get all records, receipts, and warranties about the item.
- **Act:** Go to the store and calmly tell the salesperson what you want. If that doesn't work, ask to see the supervisor or manager.
- **Contact:** If you don't receive satisfaction from the store, contact the maker of the product. Describe exactly what happened. Provide sales records and receipts if possible.

Most consumer problems can be handled by using the above steps. Just remember: Be firm and stay calm. Getting angry just gives people an excuse not to take your complaint seriously. Most businesses are eager to solve problems in a reasonable way.

21. What is the first step that you should take if you have a problem with a product that you have purchased?

_____

_____

22. What attitude should you have when making a complaint?

_____

_____

Consumer Complaints: Private Organizations

Suppose you still aren't satisfied with the laptop computer that you bought from Honest Al's. You've tried talking to the store manager. You've contacted the manufacturer. But you still can't get what you want—a replacement for your computer. The next step is to go to a private consumer assistance agency, such as the following:

Better Business Bureaus (BBBs) BBBs are private, non-profit organizations that assist consumers and businesses. BBBs provide consumers with information about harmful business practices, unsettled complaints, and other unresolved problems. They monitor advertising and selling practices. They also provide mediation and arbitration services.

Trade Associations Some industries have their own organizations to solve problems. Industries, such as banks and car manufacturers, have consumer action panels to deal with consumer complaints.

Consumer Groups Some consumer groups are controlled by consumers, not businesses. They include the Public Interest Research Group network, the Consumer's Union, and Consumers' Research, Inc. These groups not only help consumers solve problems with businesses but also help pass laws to protect consumers.

The News Media Many local and national media—magazines, newspapers, and radio/television stations and networks—have consumer features and reporters. They often investigate and expose bad products and poor business practices, as well as help consumers get their individual complaints and problems resolved.

23. How does the media help consumers?

_____

_____

Consumer Complaints: Local and State Agencies

Consumers with complaints can also contact a state, county, or city consumer office. Many local governments have a department of consumer affairs. These agencies deal with such problems as:

- faulty or harmful products that don't work or are dangerous
- false advertising that misleads
- unfair business practices or dishonest ways of doing business

Honest Al's Electronics seems to be guilty in all three areas. The computer that it sold didn't work. Also, Honest Al's advertising seemed to be part of an **unfair business practice**— a dishonest way of doing business, called "**bait and switch**." The "bait" was the low advertised price for the Z-100. It lured customers to the store where the product was "switched" to the more expensive Z-200.

24. What local government agency handles consumer complaints?

_____

_____

25. What is "bait and switch," and how did Honest Al's appear to be guilty of this violation?

_____

_____

_____

Consumer Complaints: Federal Agencies

There are many federal agencies that deal with consumer problems. They often have more power than local and state agencies. Some of the most important of these federal agencies include:

Consumer Information Center The center provides free pamphlets on such topics as health, food, buying cars, energy, and banking.

Consumer Product Safety Commission The commission protects consumers against dangerous products. It drafts regulations and makes rulings that prevent dangerous products from being sold. It can also make companies recall, or take back, such products.

U.S. Office of Consumer Affairs The Office of Consumer Affairs connects many federal programs that help consumers. It also advises the President on issues and laws that affect consumers.

26. What agency drafts regulations on consumer-related issues?

_____

Consumer Complaints: Legal Action

Imagine that you have tried everything to solve your problem with Honest Al's. You have brought your complaint to:

* the management of Honest Al's
* the manufacturer of the computer
* private consumer groups
* local and state consumer agencies
* federal consumer agencies

Your final option may be to take your case to court. If the amount involved is small, you can go to small claims court. Different states have different rules about how much money can be involved. In New

York, for example, the maximum is $3,000. Certain lawyers specialize in consumer laws. Legal Aid offices can help you get a lawyer.

27. What kinds of cases do small claims courts handle?

_____

_____

28. What organization will help you get a lawyer?

_____

_____

✔*Check Your Understanding*

Read this paragraph and answer the questions that follow.

Christina bought a CD player at Smith's Electronics. When she got the CD player home, she noticed that the forward button kept jamming. She decided to take it back, but the salesperson said that she couldn't help her.

29. What might Christina do next?

_____

_____

30. Suppose the store manager refuses to replace Christina's CD player. What should her next step be?

_____

_____

Consumer Responsibility

Suppose that you pay $100 for an autographed baseball. Later, you find out that you could have bought the same ball from someone else for $40. If the first seller didn't make any false claims, then you have no grounds for a complaint. There is generally no law against paying too much for a product. The consumer has a right to fair treatment. But it's the consumer's responsibility to shop around for the best deal.

31. What responsibility does the consumer have?

_____

_____

Reading a Product-Rating Chart

Consumer magazines test products and rate them according to quality. Its test results for personal cassette players might look something like this:

	PRICE ($)	WEIGHT (OUNCES)	FREQUENCY RESPONSE	FEATURES: RADIO	FEATURES: TAPE
SUPERSPIN	125	11	A	A	A
B-LINE	19	9	F	F	U
CIRCLESOUND	42	10	B	B	C
CLASSIC	35	10	A	B	B

A=outstanding, superior **B**=excellent **C**=good **F**=fair **U**=unsatisfactory

On the far left of the above chart is a list of several brands of portable cassette players: Superspin, B-Line, CircleSound, and Classic. The first column shows the price of each player. The second column compares the weight of each player. Column 3 rates the frequency response of each player. Finally columns 4 and 5 rate the quality of the radio and tape features in each player.

The key below the chart helps you to understand how the rating system works. An "A" rating means that the product is outstanding or superior in that category. A "B" means excellent. A "C" means good. An "F" means fair and a "U" means that the product is unsatisfactory in a particular category.

Use the ratings chart to answer the following questions.

1. Which cassette player was judged the best?

_____

2. Which cassette player had the worst radio score?

_____

3. Which cassette player had the best tape score?

_____

4. How much does CircleSound weigh?

_____

5. Which personal cassette player would you buy? Why?

_____

_____

Vocabulary

Complete each sentence with a term from the list below.

consumer rights	unfair business practices	budget
luxuries	Better Business Bureau	necessity
bait and switch	comparison shopping	

1. Food is an example of a _____ that consumers really need and must purchase.

2. Comparing prices on the same product at two or more stores is called _____.

3. _____ is an example of an unfair business practice.

4. If you have a problem with a product, the _____ _____ may be able to help you.

5. _____ are those items that are not needed but that may be wanted.

6. A _____ is a plan for spending money during a specific period of time.

7. As a consumer, you have the right not to be a victim of _____.

8. President John F. Kennedy spoke out about _____ _____.

Main Idea

Answer the following questions.

9. List ways that you can become an informed consumer.

_____

_____

10. List two rights of consumers in the United States.

_____

_____

11. Give examples of one private agency and one government agency that help consumers with their problems.

_____

_____

_____

Understanding Economics

12. Suppose you bought a cassette player and accidentally dropped it into a swimming pool. Do you think that the seller is obligated to repair it? Explain why or why not.

_____

_____

_____

13. What if the manufacturer of the cassette player from question 12 had claimed that the player was 100 percent waterproof? Would this claim change your answer to the question? Why or why not?

_____

_____

_____

14. How would you go about making a consumer complaint if you purchased a faulty product?

_____

_____

_____

Project

As a class, choose a product that you would like to rate. Then obtain several brands of this product and test them. Decide which features of the products you'd like to rate. Then make a rating chart. For example, you might rank tortilla chips according to price, weight of product, and taste. Be sure to test at least four brands of the product. Use a separate sheet of paper to record your findings.

CASE STUDY: COCA-COLA EXPANDS WORLDWIDE

Quick, can you name a soft drink that's available in more than 195 countries and asked for in more than 80 languages? You're right; it's Coca-Cola. The Coca-Cola Company is one of the world's most successful businesses. By more than a two-to-one margin, Coca-Cola outsells its closest competitor, Pepsi Cola. More than 705 million people drink Coca-Cola, but it wasn't always like that.

What's responsible for Coca-Cola's success worldwide?

Homemade Beginnings

Coca-Cola was first served over 100 years ago in an Atlanta, Georgia, pharmacy. The date was May 8, 1886. Dr. John Styth Pemberton, a local pharmacist, mixed a batch of syrup in a brass kettle in his back yard. He then took it down the street to Jacob's Pharmacy. At the pharmacy, he mixed the syrup with soda water—and Coca-Cola was born. The new product sold for 5 cents a glass as a soda fountain drink. During the rest of that year, sales of Coca-Cola averaged nine glasses per day.

More than a century later, Coca-Cola is the world's favorite soft drink. This products' growth—first in the United States and then internationally—is the result of

The first glass of Coca-Cola sold for 5 cents at an Atlanta, Georgia, pharmacy in 1886.

well-developed plans that were first laid out in the early 1900s. It was around that time that Coca-Cola was first exported to Canada. Occasional shipments also went overseas for sale in such countries as England and Germany.

Becoming a Multinational Corporation

In 1923, The Coca-Cola Company elected a new company president, Robert W. Woodruff. He established Coca-Cola's Foreign Department. This department was charged with making Coca-Cola available worldwide. By 1940, the Foreign Department had opened bottling plants in more than 45 countries. The Coca-Cola Company had now truly established itself as an international corporation, with much of its profits coming from sales in other countries.

In 1941, the United States entered World War II. The Coca-Cola Company set up bottling plants near many of the battle areas. Its goal was to make sure that any U.S. soldier who wanted to buy a Coke could do so. Its success in selling to U.S. troops overseas had an added benefit: new overseas customers developed a taste for Coke. The company

COCA-COLA'S EXPANDING GLOBAL PRESENCE

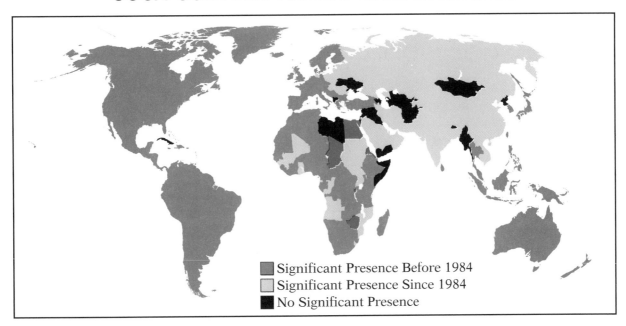

Significant Presence Before 1984
Significant Presence Since 1984
No Significant Presence

kept pushing into new markets in new countries. By the 1970s, Coca-Cola was sold mostly outside of the United States.

How did The Coca-Cola Company open up so many new markets for its product? Its growth was a result of well-developed plans and lots of hard work. The company is always trying to identify foreign markets where Coke is not sold, or where its sales are slow. It does research to find out what people in these locations are drinking and what they want. The company then carefully plans its advertising in each market to reach those specific customers.

Knowing Your Markets

In 1982, the company introduced Diet Coke. In the United States, other diet soft drinks, such as Tab, were already well established. To compete against these, the company focused on the taste of Diet Coke rather than on the fact that it had only one calorie. "Just for the taste of it" was Diet Coke's advertising slogan. In most countries outside of the United States, though, diet soft drinks were not big

sellers. In these countries, the company focused on the fact that Diet Coke had "only one calorie."

Did this strategy work? Within a year, Diet Coke was the leading diet soft drink in the United States. Within a few years, it was the third best-selling soft drink—diet or not—worldwide.

The way that Coca-Cola bottles and distributes its product has also been important to its international success. The Coca-Cola Company does not ship bottles of Coke all over the world. Nor does it own most of the Coca-Cola bottling plants around the world. Instead, Coca-Cola is bottled mostly by privately owned bottling companies.

Bottlers around the world contract with The Coca-Cola Company. The company provides the syrup to make Coca-Cola. The bottlers then make up batches of Coca-Cola, put it in bottles, and distribute those bottles locally. The company monitors the quality of this work. It also provides management and marketing training for bottlers. The company helps individual bottlers decide how best to open up new markets or to sell in existing markets. It also provides advertising worldwide.

World-Famous Advertising

More than any other single factor, advertising probably accounts for Coca-Cola's worldwide success. A study has shown that the name Coca-Cola is the most recognized soft drink brand name in the world.

Out of about 210 nations in the world, Coca-Cola is sold in almost 200 of them. The company claims that it can "actively reach out" to about 5.5 billion of the world's 6 billion citizens. Today few people have never heard of Coca-Cola.

In addition to extensive marketing research, Coca-Cola's advertising plan includes other important aspects, such as trademarks. The Coca-Cola script on a red circle has been a company trademark for more than a century. The contoured glass bottle has been in use for more than 80 years and is instantly recognized as a Coke bottle. It is also a registered trademark with the U.S. Patent Office. This means that no other company can legally use that shape of bottle.

The Coca-Cola Company has always spent large amounts on advertising. In doing so, it has used some of the best talents available. For example, the famous American artist, Norman Rockwell, painted advertisements for Coca-Cola for many years.

Another factor that helped Coca-Cola achieve huge international success is its sponsorship of the Olympics. The company has been involved with the games since 1928. It now supports Olympic teams in more than 180 countries. Such support, along with the local ownership of Coca-Cola bottling

Thanks to ad campaigns like this one featuring its Olympic Bear, Coca-Cola boasts the best brand-name recognition in the world.

plants, helps people in other countries feel that Coca-Cola is not just an American company, but also a local company.

Reaching for New Markets

The Coca-Cola empire continues to grow. It has recently opened plants in Vietnam and Fiji. In the late 1990s, the company plans to open ten bottling plants in China. Coca-Cola is already one of the largest U.S. investors in that country.

Creating a multinational corporation also takes political awareness. When the Berlin Wall fell in 1989, Coca-Cola was one of the first Western companies to start selling products in eastern Germany. Many countries that were previously communist, such as East Germany and Russia, had not allowed any private businesses to operate freely before the early 1990s. Once the opportunity to trade in these countries became available, The Coca-Cola Company poured its resources into these areas.

Coca-Cola was also one of the first U.S. companies to establish business in Vietnam. Because of U.S. involvement in the Vietnam War, the U.S. government did not allow any companies to do business in Vietnam before 1995.

What does all of this international success mean for The Coca-Cola Company? It means record profits, 80 percent of them from foreign markets. It also means that stockholders have the potential to make lots of money.

For example, suppose you had bought $1,000 worth of Coca-Cola stock in 1984. If you had reinvested all the dividends it earned, then that stock would have been worth about $12,000 ten years later. Even that amazing 1,100 percent gain is small compared to the growth of Coca-Cola's original stock. The company issued stock in 1919 at $40 a share. Today one of those $40 shares of Coca-Cola would be worth about $2.5 million. Only an international company could have created that kind of growth through the years.

Eighty percent of Coca-Cola's profits come from foreign markets like China, where the company is one of the largest U.S. investors.

International Trade

As you just learned, Coca-Cola is one of the most successful international businesses in the world. It is by no means, however, the first company to be successful selling worldwide. As long as there have been nations, there has been trade between them.

Long ago, the Roman Empire was the center of a huge trade network. Rome got wild animals from Great Britain. From Egypt, it received grain. Silks and spices came from the Far East. What did Rome trade in return? It traded jewelry, fine pottery, olive oil, and glass. Trade between nations, or between companies of different nations, is called **international trade**.

International trade started thousands of years ago with the movement of valuable goods across continents. Marco Polo opened trade routes when he traveled to the Far East in the 14th century. Reports of his travels fascinated Europeans. Ships began carrying precious stones, spices, silk, and other goods between China and Venice, Italy, where Polo lived.

Interest in acquiring foreign goods has brought historic tragedies. For example, the Aztec civilization, in what is now Mexico, was conquered and destroyed in the 16th century by Spanish traders intent on bringing home gold.

1. What is international trade?

_____

_____

2. What have been some side effects of international trade?

_____

_____

Why International Trade?

Each country specializes in the production of certain goods and services. **Specialization** refers to a country's focusing on producing one product or a few products rather than producing everything to satisfy its wants and needs. Because no two nations have the same set of natural resources, human resources, or capital resources, what one country can produce best is different from what another country can produce best.

For example, the United States has rich soil and a good climate for growing some of the best wheat in the world. It also has farmers who are expert at growing wheat, and it has the capital to manufacture farm machinery.

On the other hand, the United States does not have the right soil or climate to grow coffee, but Brazil does. Therefore, the United States can efficiently sell wheat to Brazil, and Brazil can efficiently sell coffee to the United States. Because each country can produce some products more efficiently than others, trade between these two countries results in advantages that benefit both countries.

International trade has been growing rapidly throughout the world. It is not uncommon today to walk into a supermarket and find fruit from Israel, Jamaica, and Costa Rica; ham from Italy; and cheeses from France, Greece, and Spain. This is a result of international trade among many nations throughout the world.

3. Why do different countries produce different goods?

_____

_____

4. Why is trade among different countries beneficial to all the countries involved?

_____

_____

Advances in communication and transportation have made international trade easier in the twentieth century. As a result, buyers and sellers don't even have to meet. Buying and selling can be done via telephones, facsimile machines, and computers.

Easier international trade means that foreign producers can readily compete against domestic producers. Through most of this century, for example, most cars sold in the United States were made by one of three U.S. companies: Ford, Chrysler, or General Motors. The "Big Three" dominated the market. During the 1970s, however, that changed. Oil shortages made gasoline prices jump sharply. Suddenly, smaller and more fuel-efficient cars became attractive to American car buyers. Japanese companies sold such cars. Americans started to buy Japanese cars almost faster than Japanese companies could deliver them.

The Japanese market share for automobiles grew rapidly. **Market share** is the percentage of a market held or controlled by one company or one country. For example, if Honda sells 35% of all cars bought in the United States this year, then Honda's U.S. market share would be 35%. Fifteen years passed before the Big Three started to regain the market share that they had lost to international competition.

5. What are two factors that have made international trade easier in the 20th century?

_____

_____

6. What is market share?

_____

_____

TAKE ANOTHER LOOK

The pie graph below shows the American soft-drink market.

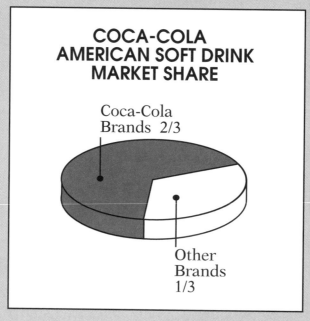

COCA-COLA
AMERICAN SOFT DRINK
MARKET SHARE

Coca-Cola Brands 2/3

Other Brands 1/3

7. What is Coca-Cola's share of the American soft-drink market?

_____

_____

As you read earlier, a nation tends to specialize in what it produces most efficiently. For example, the French economy specializes in cheese. As a result, the French export a large amount of cheese.

Exports are goods sold to other countries. Most of a country's exports will be from its areas of specialization. Most of a country's imports, on the other hand, will be products outside of its specialization. **Imports** are goods bought from another country.

8. What is meant by a country's specialization?

_____

_____

9. What are exports?

_____

_____

10. What are imports?

_____

_____

Absolute Advantage and Comparative Advantage

Countries specialize in certain products. That specialization gives them advantages in trade. For example, because Jamaica contains one of the world's largest natural supplies of bauxite, it is one of the world's leading exporters of this metal. Jamaica is said to have absolute advantage over most other countries in exporting this metal, which is used to produce aluminum. **Absolute advantage** results when a nation can produce more of a product than another nation can, even though both use the same amount of resources. Why this may occur is that a country's resources may be better suited to the production of that good, or it has more expertise producing the good.

What is important for international trade, however, is when a country has a comparative advantage over another country. **Comparative advantage** occurs when a nation can produce a product at a lower opportunity cost than its trading partner. As you learned in Chapter 1, opportunity cost, or alternative cost, is what must be given up in order to have something else. Every economic decision has an opportunity cost.

Let's look at Zimbabwe in Africa. Zimbabwe has an increasing population. This population increase means that every year the country has more people to feed. It also has excellent growing conditions for producing a number of crops. Zimbabwe's leaders must make choices, however, about which crops to grow. It is essential to export items for which Zimbabwe will receive the best value.

Zimbabwe's leaders have decided that the country will receive the best value if it grows and exports cut flowers to Europe, and imports food products from other countries. There is a big market for flowers in European countries, especially in the Netherlands in northern Europe.

Even though the Netherlands can grow cut flowers, Zimbabwe can grow them more efficiently at a lower cost. Therefore, Zimbabwe has a comparative advantage over the Netherlands in flower production. People in the Netherlands benefit because they can buy flowers from Zimbabwe more cheaply than growing them themselves. Zimbabwe also benefits if it exports flowers to the Netherlands. With the money it receives, Zimbabwe can purchase food from a country that produces food more efficiently than it could. Consumers in Zimbabwe are better off because they will pay less for the imported food.

11. What is absolute advantage?

_____

_____

12. What is comparative advantage?

_____

_____

13. Why did Zimbabwe decide to specialize in flower production?

_____

_____

14. Explain how consumers in Zimbabwe could indirectly benefit from the exporting of flowers.

_____

_____

Foreign Currency and Exchange Rates

When Coca-Cola sells its soft drinks in India, people pay for their drinks in Indian money called *rupees*. In order to use that money in the United States, Coca-Cola must change the rupees into dollars. This exchange of foreign money, or foreign currency, is done in foreign exchange markets. These markets trade one foreign currency for another. They will trade so many rupees, for example, for one dollar. An important question would be "How many rupees for a dollar?"

Until the 1970s, major trading nations agreed to exchange fixed rates. A **fixed exchange rate** refers to a government's setting the value of its currency against a single standard, or a set price. Traders could then compute equivalents between any two currencies.

Today the United States and its major trading parties use flexible exchange rates. With a **flexible exchange rate**, the value of each currency is decided by supply and demand. For example, if there is increased demand for U.S. goods, there will be increased demand for U.S. dollars. Increased demand for dollars will make dollars more expensive. This means that on one day 25 rupees may buy a dollar. The next day it may take 27.5 rupees to buy a dollar.

15. How is a fixed exchange rate different from a flexible exchange rate?

_____

_____

_____

Think About It!

The chart below is a foreign currency exchange rate chart that you might see in a bank. Look carefully at the exchange rates in the two columns.

FOREIGN CURRENCY EXCHANGE RATES

Currency	Bank buys at	Bank sells at
Canada (Can $)	$ 0.785	$ 0.815
England (pound)	$ 1.551	$ 1.610
Japan (yen)	$ 0.0112	$ 0.0125

16. How does the bank make a profit when it exchanges currency?

_____

_____

Multinational Corporations

The Coca-Cola Company is one of the world's largest corporations. It is a multinational corporation—sometimes just called a multinational. **Multinational corporations** are large corporations that do business in many countries. A number of companies will often be owned by one multinational corporation. These companies are known as **subsidiaries** of the corporation that owns them.

When The Coca-Cola Company began doing business in Egypt, for example, it started an Egyptian subsidiary. That company is based in Cairo, Egypt, and is largely staffed by Egyptians. The Coca-Cola Company sells its syrup to the Cairo subsidiary. The subsidiary then mixes the syrup with soda water, bottles it, and sells it in Egypt.

When a multinational moves into a new country, it will often set up a joint venture with an established company from that country. The joint venture is a type of partnership. Each company contributes elements to the product, and each gets some of the profit. For example, Coca-Cola set up a joint venture in 1995 with a company in Vietnam to make and distribute Coca-Cola.

17. What is a multinational corporation?

_____

_____

18. Describe a joint venture between a U.S. company and a foreign company.

_____

_____

✔ *Check Your Understanding*

Suppose you are working for The Coca-Cola Company and have just agreed to a joint venture with Refresk, Inc., a soft drink manufacturer in the Czech Republic. Together, the two companies are going to bottle and distribute Coca-Cola in that country.

19. What resources do you think each company might contribute to the partnership?

_____

_____

_____

Free Trade or Restricted Trade?

Free trade is open business competition among nations without restrictions imposed by individual countries. Most economists see many advantages to free trade. When countries specialize where they have a comparative advantage and trade with each other, resources are used efficiently. This means that more goods and services can be produced by both countries. Then, when two countries trade freely, people in both countries can consume more than they could consume without trade.

People benefit from trade in many ways. Trade enables people to consume a wider variety of goods and services. Imagine how your choices would be limited if you could only purchase products made in the United States.

Free trade also allows consumers to buy goods at lower prices. For example, car tires can be produced more cheaply in Canada and car radios can be produced more cheaply in the United States. When Canadian tires are traded for U.S. radios, consumers in both countries can benefit. People in the U.S. can buy lower-priced tires. People in Canada can buy lower-priced radios.

Despite its advantages, however, free trade often does not take place. Countries can be protective of their own industries and restrict foreign industries. Governments often try to limit the quantities of foreign-made goods sold in their country. There are three major reasons for this:

- protection of domestic jobs
- protection of "infant industries"
- protection of national security

Protection of Domestic Jobs Domestic means relating to, or within, one's own country. When citizens buy foreign goods rather than domestic goods, domestic industry may suffer and domestic jobs may be lost. For example, when Japanese cars became popular in the United States, sales of U.S.-made autos dropped. Many U.S. auto workers eventually lost their jobs. To counteract this type of situation, governments sometimes impose restrictions on the import of foreign goods.

Protection of "Infant Industries" An **infant industry** is an industry that is just becoming established in a country. Some people think that certain newly developing industries should be protected from more established foreign competition. When new companies start up, they are usually less efficient than more established companies. This inefficiency may initially cause a new company to charge higher prices than its competitors. A country may support an infant industry even though its prices might be a bit higher than those of foreign competitors. This support gives the infant industry time to become more efficient and competitive.

Protection of National Security Certain goods and services are vital to a nation's defense. In times of war, countries want these goods and services to be produced domestically. If they are produced by foreign companies, supplies of them may be cut off. Governments often restrict imports of items that would compete with industries that are important to their national defense.

20. What are three reasons that nations might restrict imports?

_____

_____

_____

How Do Governments Restrict Trade?

Governments use three primary tools to restrict foreign trade:

- tariffs

- quotas

- embargoes

Tariffs Taxes that governments impose on imported goods are called tariffs. Tariffs may be collected simply for the sake of making money for the government. They were a primary source of income for the U.S. government in the 19th century. Today, however, tariffs are usually imposed to raise the cost of foreign goods. The consumer who must pay the price of the tariff will often find the foreign item too expensive and will buy a domestic item instead. This is one way that governments try to protect domestic industry from foreign competition.

Quotas Limits on the value or number of a certain item that can be imported are called **quotas**. For example, a government may try to help its domestic textile industry by putting quotas on the number of yards of textiles that the country can import. Limiting foreign goods coming into a country limits the amount of competition that domestic industries face.

Embargoes Complete restriction of the import—or the export—of certain goods to a country is an **embargo**. For example, because of the Vietnam War, the United States imposed a trade embargo against North Vietnam in 1964. That embargo was not lifted by the United States until 1994. No goods from that country could legally enter the United States. No U.S. goods could be exported legally to Vietnam.

Embargoes are usually imposed for political or national defense reasons. The Vietnam embargo was continued by the United States for 30 years because it believed that Vietnam was not providing full information on U.S. POWs (prisoners of war) and MIAs (soldiers declared missing in action).

21. What are three ways that a country might restrict trade?

_____

_____

_____

22. How are quotas and embargoes alike?

_____

_____

23. How are quotas and embargoes different?

_____

_____

Agreements on International Trade

Although some people want nations to have barriers to limit trade, other people want nations to relax some of those barriers. In recent years, countries interested in removing restrictions on free trade have signed treaties and agreements to do just that.

One such agreement is the **North American Free Trade Agreement** (NAFTA). The North American Free Trade Agreement is a trade agreement among Canada, the United States, and Mexico that was signed in 1995. It essentially removes all tariffs, quotas, and other barriers to free trade among these nations. The goal of NAFTA is to make, for example, trade between the United States and Mexico as barrier-free as trade between California and New York.

24. What is the purpose of NAFTA?

_____

_____

As with any agreement, there are pros and cons to NAFTA. People who are for this agreement believe that it will stimulate American businesses and, therefore, the economy by increasing the trade of goods and resources among these three countries. They say that

NAFTA will allow larger quantities of capital, materials, goods, and services to move among them with less government control. An example of NAFTA's benefits to its participants might be the importing of high quality milk from the United States to Mexico. NAFTA supporters claim that this helps U.S. dairies increase earnings while improving Mexican children's health.

Opponents of NAFTA argue that what this treaty does is send billions of Canadian and U.S. dollars directly to Mexico. Labor is cheaper in Mexico. This means that some U.S. workers may lose their jobs. There are also very loose environmental and safety standards in Mexico. There are certain cities in Mexico where the air, water, and soil are already contaminated because multinational giants have built factories there. As a result of the opposition against NAFTA, negotiators attached side agreements to the overall agreement. Review panels have been set up to judge whether each nation's rights to establish its own laws are being infringed upon by enforcement of the treaty.

25. Why are some people in favor of NAFTA?

_____

_____

26. Why are some people against NAFTA?

_____

_____

Another trade treaty is the General Agreement on Tariffs and Trade (GATT). GATT is similar to NAFTA except that it is a worldwide agreement. Its goal is to remove all tariffs and restrictions on goods entering and leaving its member nations. The first GATT was signed in 1947 by 23 nations. Since then, the treaty has been renegotiated every few years. Today there are more than 80 member nations. The **General Agreement on Tariffs and Trade** is an agreement that provides for much freer trade among many of the world's nations.

27. What is GATT?

_____

_____

28. How does GATT differ from NAFTA?

_____

_____

Reading a Picture Graph

In the graph below, each Coke bottle stands for about 500 million cases of Coca-Cola sold. Half a symbol stands for about 250 million cases sold; three quarters of a symbol stands for about 375 million cases sold.

1994 COCA-COLA SALES BY WORLD REGION

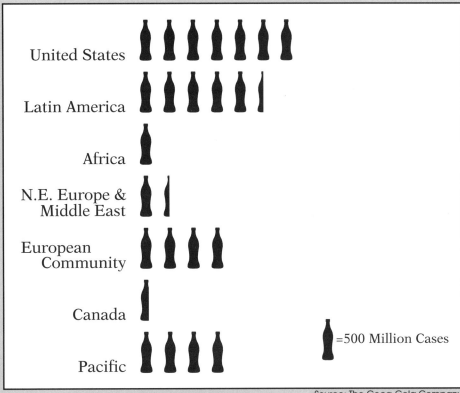

Source: The Coca-Cola Company

Use the graph to answer the following questions.

1. About how many cases were sold in the European Community?

_____

2. About how many cases were sold in Canada?

_____

3. In which two regions were about the same number of cases sold?

_____

4. By looking at this graph, which countries do you think will have increased sales in the coming years? Explain.

_____

5. About how many cases were sold in all in 1994?

_____

Vocabulary

Complete each sentence with a term from the list below.

absolute advantage	quotas	embargoes	GATT
comparative advantage	exports	free trade	
fixed exchange rate	imports	NAFTA	

1. _____ are goods bought from suppliers in another country.

2. _____ are limits on the value or number of certain items that can be imported.

3. A nation has a(n) _____ if it can produce more of a product than another nation can using the same amount of resources.

4. _____ are complete restrictions on imports and exports by a certain country.

5. _____ are goods sold to another country.

6. _____ is open business competition among nations without restrictions imposed by individual countries.

7. _____ stands for the General Agreement on Tariffs and Trade.

8. With a(n) _____, each government sets the value of its currency against a single standard.

9. _____ is an agreement that removes all tariffs, quotas, and other barriers to free trade among Canada, the United States, and Mexico.

10. _____ occurs when a country can produce a product at a lower opportunity cost than its trading partner.

Main Idea

Answer the following questions.

11. Explain how specialization affects international trade.

_____

_____

12. What are some of the barriers to international trade?

_____

_____

13. List one reason that people want international trade restricted?

_____

_____

Understanding Economics

14. Think about a product you buy that is made by a foreign company. What is the product? In which country is the product made? Are there any domestic companies that make a similar product? If so, why did you choose the foreign-made product?

_____

_____

_____

15. Choose a product for a foreign market. What product would you try to sell? Why? In what foreign market would you try to sell it? Why?

_____

_____

_____

Project

Work with a group and choose a multinational corporation to research. Find out what the corporation sells and to which countries it sells its products. Look up the corporation's sales record. Present your group's findings in a short report. Use graphs and other visual aids.

GLOSSARY

Absolute advantage results when a nation can produce more of a product than another nation using the same amount of resources (171)

Alternative cost also called opportunity cost, the sacrifice made in an economic decision; what is given up when you must make a choice (16)

"Bait and switch" the unfair business practice of attracting customers with a low priced item and then switching it with a higher priced item (158)

Bank a financial institution that accepts savings, makes loans, and provides checking accounts (120)

Bank statement a monthly record of transactions in a bank account (122)

Barter the direct trading of one good for another (114)

Bear market a period of generally declining stock prices (140)

Blue-collar workers laborers who generally perform physical work (96)

Board of directors people elected by some stockholders to make decisions about a corporation (82)

Bond an interest-bearing certificate issued by a corporation or a government that can be cashed in by a specific date (83)

Broker a middle person who buys and sells stocks and bonds for groups and individuals (135)

Budget a plan for spending money over a specific period of time (153)

Bull market a period of generally increasing stock prices (140)

Business cycle cycle of alternating strong and weak periods in the economy (68)

Buyers people who buy products; consumers (29)

Buying power amount of goods and services that money will purchase (117)

Capital gains profits made from the sale or trading of an investment, such as stock shares (133)

Capital loss loss from the sale of an investment (134)

Capital resources goods made by people that are used to create other goods and services (12)

Capitalism an economic system in which individuals own and control the factors of production (26)

Certificates of deposit (CDs) a type of savings account in which money can be drawn only after a period of time or else there is a penalty (120)

Charter a state license, for example, allowing a business to be a corporation (80)

Chief executive officer (CEO) a person who carries out decisions made by the board of directors of a corporation (82)

Command economic system an economic system in which a central agency owns and controls the factors of production and decides what goods the country will produce and distribute (26)

Commodity money money that is valuable in itself (117)

Common stocks stocks that do not guarantee to pay dividends; stockholders have voting rights (134)

Comparative advantage occurs when a nation can produce a product at a lower opportunity cost than its trading partner (171)

Comparison shopping the comparing of prices on the same product at two or more stores (154)

Competition a rivalry between producers or sellers who sell similar products (33)

Consumer Price Index compares average prices of selected goods and services in one year with those of an earlier, or base, year (70)

Consumer rights laws that protect people against loss or harm from products (156)

Consumers people who buy goods and services to satisfy their wants and needs; buyers (30)

Corporate taxes a tax representing the percentage of profits that corporations pay the federal government (66)

Corporation a business owned by its stockholders (79)

Cost what a person gives up, or sacrifices, when he or she makes an economic choice (16)

Cost of living the price of basic needs, such as food, clothing, and housing (105)

Currency coins and paper money; fiat money (118)

Deflation a sustained fall in the average level of prices in a whole economy (70)

Demand the amount of goods and services that people are willing and able to buy at different prices (41)

Demand curve points connected on a graph showing how much of an item people are willing to buy at different prices (42)

Direct taxes taxes imposed directly on the taxpayer, such as an income tax (66)

Discrimination to judge someone for qualities other than skill (104)

Dividend a portion of a corporation's profits that is distributed among its stockholders (83)

Divisible capable of being divided into smaller parts (116)

Dow Jones Industrial Average records the average performance of a large group of selected industrial stocks (140)

Economic freedom allows individuals to make economic decisions that they believe are in their own best interest (31)

Economic system the way in which a society decides how to use its resources to produce and distribute goods and services (24)

Economics the study of how people use limited resources to produce goods and services (7)

Elastic demand occurs when a relatively small price change affects the amount, or quantity, that people are willing to buy (43)

Elastic supply occurs when a relatively small change in price creates a large change in the amount that producers are willing to supply (49)

Embargo a complete restriction on certain imports and exports (176)

Entrepreneurs people who start new businesses and introduce new products (11)

Equilibrium price the price at which amount demanded equals the amount supplied (51)

Exchange the trading of goods and services (114)

Excise taxes taxes on goods, such as gasoline and tobacco; indirect taxes (66)

Expenses costs; for example, the financial costs of running a business (78)

Exports goods sold to other countries (171)

Factors of production resources that people use to create goods and services; also called productive resources (11)

Federal Reserve System the central banking system of the United States; "The Fed" (122)

Fiat money money made valuable by government order (118)

Financial capital money needed to start a business or for other investment purposes (78)

Fixed costs costs that a producer must pay to stay in business, such as rent and insurance (49)

Fixed exchange rate when a government sets the value of its currency against a single standard, or a set price (172)

Flexible exchange rate the value of a nation's currency is decided by supply and demand (173)

Fraud the act of people lying about themselves or a product to make a profit (63)

Free trade the open trade among nations without restrictions made by individual countries (174)

General Agreement on Tariffs and Trade (GATT) an agreement that provides for much freer trade among many nations (178)

General mutual funds a mutual fund that invests in securities from diverse business sectors (138)

General partnership a business in which partners share decisions, profits, and losses (79)

General welfare the well-being of all citizens (61)

Goods products that people use (7)

Government bonds notes representing loans that the government promises to pay back with interest (123)

Gross Domestic Product a measure of how much an economy produces (68)

Gross pay the total amount of money earned before deductions are subtracted (105)

Human resources the physical and mental labor and skills and ideas that people use to produce goods and services (11)

Imports goods bought from another country (171)

Income taxes taxes on income paid to federal, state, and some city governments by anyone working in the United States (65)

Indirect taxes taxes not directly imposed on the one who pays the tax; for example, taxes on items bought (66)

Inelastic demand occurs when a change in price has relatively little affect on the amount that people are willing to buy (43)

Inelastic supply occurs when a change in price has relatively little effect on the amount that producers are willing to supply (49)

Infant industry an industry that is just becoming established in a country (175)

Inflation a sustained increase in the average level of prices in the whole economy (64)

Interest money paid for the use of someone else's money (79)

International trade the trade between nations or between companies of different nations (168)

Investment the act of using money to get a profit in the future (131)

Investors people who use money to make a profit in the future (78)

Labor workers who work for a business (11)

Labor force total number of people over the age of 16 who are employed or are actively seeking work (96)

Labor unions groups of workers banded together (103)

Law of demand states that as prices of goods increase, people are willing to buy less; as prices decrease, people are willing to buy more (41)

Law of supply states that as prices of goods rise, producers will be willing to make more goods; as prices fall producers will be willing to make fewer goods (47)

Limited partnership a business in which the partner often does not make decisions and is often responsible only for the amount of money invested in the business (79)

Loss when a business' income is less than its costs (32)

Luxuries items that are not needed but are wanted; non-necessities (150)

Macroeconomics the study of the economy as a whole (9)

Market the actions of buying and selling (29)

Market economic system an economic system in which individuals and businesses decide what to produce and how to produce and distribute goods and services; free enterprise; capitalism (26)

Market share the percentage of a market held or controlled by one company or one country (169)

Microeconomics the study of economic decision-making by individuals and businesses (8)

Mixed economic system an economic system that includes some features from market, traditional, and command economic systems (28)

Money something that can be used to buy all types of goods and services (114)

Money market mutual fund a mutual fund that invests in money market certificates (142)

Money supply total value of currency and checkable deposits in the economy (121)

Monopoly exists when a single seller sells a product (85)

Multinational corporations large corporations that do business in many countries (173)

Mutual fund a company that pools together the investment monies of many people and then invests those monies in stocks and bonds (131)

Natural resources resources that are found in nature (11)

Near money goods that are almost, but not exactly, like money (119)

Necessities items that are really needed, such as food, clothing, and housing; needs (150)

Needs items that people cannot do without; necessities (9)

Net pay the amount of money left after deductions are subtracted (105)

Non-necessities items that are not needed but are wanted; luxuries (150)

Nonrenewable resources natural resources that cannot be replaced (11)

North American Free Trade Agreement (NAFTA) a trade agreement among Canada, Mexico, and the United States (177)

Oligopoly occurs when a few competitors dominate a market (87)

Partnership a business owned by two or more people (79)

Passbook account a savings account in which money can be withdrawn at any time (120)

Patent a license issued by the federal government to an inventor that gives him or her total rights over an invention (87)

Pay stub a record of a worker's gross pay and deductions for a particular pay period (107)

Pension money paid regularly to a person upon his or her retirement (106)

Perfect competition occurs when no one buyer or seller has control over the price of a good (84)

Personal checks represent money in a person's checking account at a bank (118)

Preferred stocks stocks that guarantee stockholders dividends; stockholders have no voting rights in the company (134)

Price amount of money asked or paid for a good or service (31)

Private property property owned by businesses or individuals, not by the government (33)

Producers people who create goods and services (30)

Product market the market for goods and services; consumers pay money to producers for products (30)

Production the sum total of all the methods that a company uses to create goods and services (13)

Production cost the total amount of money it takes to make a product (49)

Productive resources capital, human, and natural resources used to create goods and services; also called factors of production (11)

Professionals workers with a lot of training and education; white-collar workers (96)

Profit money made by a business after all costs, or expenses, have been paid; money gained from the sale or trading of an investment (32)

Profit motive the search for the greatest profit (32)

Progressive tax a tax in which individuals who earn more money pay a higher percentage of their income (65)

Public facilities and services programs provided by the government, such as national defense, education, and some health care (60)

Quotas limits on the value or number of certain imported goods (176)

Regressive tax a tax in which individuals who earn less money pay a higher percentage of their income (66)

Renewable resource a natural resource that can be replaced (11)

Representative money money that stands for, or represents, something else of value, such as personal checks and traveler's checks (118)

Resource market producers pay individuals for productive resources that they need to make products (30)

Risk the chance of losing something valuable (80)

Savings account an account at a bank in which a person deposits his or her money in order to earn interest; an example of near money (119)

Savings and loan associations financial institutions similar to banks (120)

Scarcity occurs when people want more goods and services than they can have (8)

Sector mutual funds a mutual fund that invests in securities in a specific business sector, such as the technology sector (138)

Securities stocks and bonds (131)

Sellers people who sell products; producers (29)

Services activities that people do for other people (7)

Share a unit of stock representing ownership of a corporation (83)

Shortage occurs when people want to buy more of a good than is available at a given price (52)

Skill level the level of training and schooling of a worker (99)

Sole proprietor a person who owns and runs a business alone (79)

Specialization when a person or country focuses on producing one product or a few products (168)

Speculation the practice of engaging in high risk business transactions in the hope of making a high return (133)

Stock a share of ownership in a corporation (83)

Stock exchanges marketplaces where stocks are bought and sold (135)

Stock split occurs when two or more shares of stock are given for every one share owned (135)

Stockholders people who own shares of stock in a corporation; owners of a corporation (79)

Subsidiaries companies owned by a larger, sometimes multinational, corporation (173)

Supply how much producers are willing and able to sell at different prices (47)

Supply curve points on a graph that show that a producer's willingness to supply a product increases with price (48)

Surplus occurs when there is too much of a good available at a given price (52)

Tariff federal government tax on imported goods (67)

Taxes monies collected by governments from individuals and businesses (61)

Trade-off occurs when one choice is exchanged for another (15)

Tradition-based economic system an economic system in which decisions are based largely on custom (24)

Traveler's checks checks that represent money that a person has previously paid to a large bank or company (118)

Unemployment occurs when people are willing and able to work but can't find jobs (64)

Unfair business practice a dishonest way to do business (158)

Variable costs the costs that change as production increases or decreases, such as raw material costs and wages (50)

Voluntary exchange occurs when people trade freely with one another (31)

Wants items that people desire but do not need (9)

White-collar workers people who generally perform "mental work"; professionals (96)